THE
HISTORY OF
THE PHILIPPINES

ADVISORY BOARD

THE
HISTORY OF
THE PHILIPPINES

Kathleen Nadeau

The Greenwood Histories of the Modern Nations
Frank W. Thackeray and John E. Findling, Series Editors

Greenwood Press
Westport, Connecticut • London

Library of Congress Cataloging-in-Publication Data

Nadeau, Kathleen M., 1952–
    The history of the Philippines / Kathleen Nadeau.
        p. cm. — (The Greenwood histories of the modern nations, ISSN 1096–2905)
    Includes bibliographical references and index.
    ISBN 978–0–313–34090–1 (alk. paper)
    1. Philippines—History.   I. Title.
    DS668.N33   2008
    959.9—dc22   2008012985

British Library Cataloguing in Publication Data is available.

Library of Congress Catalog Card Number: 2008012985
ISBN: 978–0–313–34090–1
ISSN: 1096–2905

First published in 2008

Greenwood Press, 88 Post Road West, Westport, CT 06881
An imprint of Greenwood Publishing Group, Inc.
www.greenwood.com

Printed in the United States of America

The paper used in this book complies with the
Permanent Paper Standard issued by the National
Information Standards Organization (Z39.48–1984).

10 9 8 7 6 5 4 3 2 1

Contents

Series Foreword

The *Greenwood Histories of the Modern Nations* series is intended to provide students and interested laypeople with up-to-date, concise, and analytical histories of many of the nations of the contemporary world. Not since the 1960s has there been a systematic attempt to publish a series of national histories, and, as editors, we believe that this series will prove to be a valuable contribution to our understanding of other countries in our increasingly interdependent world.

Over thirty years ago, at the end of the 1960s, the Cold War was an accepted reality of global politics, the process of decolonization was still in progress, the idea of a unified Europe with a single currency was unheard of, the United States was mired in a war in Vietnam, and the economic boom of Asia was still years in the future. Richard Nixon was president of the United States, Mao Tse-tung (not yet Mao Zedong) ruled China, Leonid Brezhnev guided the Soviet Union, and Harold Wilson was prime minister of the United Kingdom. Authoritarian dictators still ruled most of Latin America, the Middle East was reeling in the wake of the Six-Day War, and Shah Reza Pahlavi was at the height of his power in Iran. Clearly, the past 30 years have been witness to a great deal of historical change, and it is to this change that this series is primarily addressed.

With the help of a distinguished advisory board, we have selected nations whose political, economic, and social affairs mark them as among the most important in the waning years of the twentieth century, and for each nation we have found an author who is recognized as a specialist in the history of that nation. These authors have worked most cooperatively with us and with Greenwood Press to produce volumes that reflect current research on their nations and that are interesting and informative to their prospective readers.

The importance of a series such as this cannot be underestimated. As a superpower whose influence is felt all over the world, the United States can claim a "special" relationship with almost every other nation. Yet many Americans know very little about the histories of the nations with which the United States relates. How did they get to be the way they are? What kind of political systems have evolved there? What kind of influence do they have in their own region? What are the dominant political, religious, and cultural forces that move their leaders? These and many other questions are answered in the volumes of this series.

The authors who have contributed to this series have written comprehensive histories of their nations, dating back to prehistoric times in some cases. Each of them, however, has devoted a significant portion of the book to events of the last thirty years, because the modern era has contributed the most to contemporary issues that have an impact on U.S. policy. Authors have made an effort to be as up-to-date as possible so that readers can benefit from the most recent scholarship and a narrative that includes very recent events.

In addition to the historical narrative, each volume in this series contains an introductory overview of the country's geography, political institutions, economic structure, and cultural attributes. This is designed to give readers a picture of the nation as it exists in the contemporary world. Each volume also contains additional chapters that add interesting and useful detail to the historical narrative. One chapter is a thorough chronology of important historical events, making it easy for readers to follow the flow of a particular nation's history. Another chapter features biographical sketches of the nation's most important figures in order to humanize some of the individuals who have contributed to the historical development of their nation. Each volume also contains a comprehensive bibliography, so that those readers whose interest has been sparked may find out more about the nation and its history. Finally, there is a carefully prepared topic and person index.

Readers of these volumes will find them fascinating to read and useful in understanding the contemporary world and the nations that comprise it. As series editors, it is our hope that this series will contribute to a heightened sense of global understanding as we embark on a new century.

Frank W. Thackeray and John E. Findling
Indiana University Southeast

Acknowledgments

The author is grateful to her colleagues, especially in the Philippine Studies Group of the Association for Asian Studies, USA, and in the Philippines and around the world, whose friendship and sincere devotion to promoting Philippine studies continues to be an inspiration. Special thanks to those whose works are cited in the bibliographic essay at the end of this text. I would like to thank my many colleagues at California State University, San Bernardino, especially those with whom I work and whom I have come to know and value. Thanks to my students whose passion, discipline, and positive attitude in class keeps me going. A book like this would not be complete without thanking my Filipino American students whose dedication to learning more about and promoting their rich cultural and historical heritage is of great benefit to the world community of which we are all part. Finally, I would like to thank my editors for their help in pushing this project through to completion and my parents for their encouragement.

0 100 200 km
0 100 200 mi

Luzon
Strait

Babuyan
Islands

Aparri

Luzon

San Fernando

Baguio

*South
China
Sea*

Angeles

Quezon CIty

MANILA

Batangas

*Philippine
Sea*

Legaspi

Mindoro

Samar

Panay

Iloilo

Bacolod

Leyte

Palawan

Cebu

Gulmaras
Island

Puerto
Princesa

Negros

Butuan

Cagayan
de Oro

Iligan

Sulu Sea

Mindanao

Davao

Zamboanga

Jolo

Basilan

*Celebes
Sea*

INDONESIA

Philippines. Adapted from Bookcomp, Inc.

Introduction

The present-day Philippines is an archipelago nation of more than 7,100 islands, with a coastline that stretches 10,850 miles, which is twice the length of the coastline of California. The archipelago lies off the southeast coast of the Asian mainland between Borneo and Taiwan. It is surrounded in the west by the South China Sea, in the east by the Pacific Ocean, in the south by the Sulu and Celebes seas, and in the north by the Bashi Channel. These tropical and mountainous islands have a land area of 115,831 square miles.[1] The country is composed of three major regions: Luzon, the largest island in the north; the Visayas, an island group in the center; and Mindanao, the largest island in the south. These regions have distinct political, social, and cultural differences. The capital is Manila in Luzon. Other important cities are Cebu, in the Visayas; Davao, Cotobato, and Zamboanga, in Mindanao; and Jolo, in the Sulu archipelago of Mindanao.

The climate is always tropical and warm because of the Philippines' location, 5 to 20 degrees north of the equator. There are two main seasons: the dry season lasts from March to June, and the monsoon season from July to October. The intervening months of November to February are wonderfully warm with a soothing sea breeze. The archipelago lays on the edge of the so-called Ring of Fire, a chain of active volcanoes marking the intersection of two tectonic plates, which makes the possibility of an earthquake or volcanic eruption an ever-present danger. The worst recorded calamity occurred in June 1991, when Mount Pinatubo, in central Luzon, blew up, causing widespread devastation. Typhoons, annually lash out at the islands, especially those closest to the Pacific. Because of deforestation, even a mild typhoon can now cause flash flooding and tragic loss of human life and property, such as happened when typhoon Uring hit Ormoc, Leyte, on November 5, 1991.[2]

The land of the Philippines is characterized by irregular coasts, alluvial plains, narrow valleys, and rolling hills and mountains running north to south. It used to have a lush and tropical forest cover with a diverse ecosystem. However, deforestation reduced the forests to only 19.4 percent by the end of the twentieth century.[3] Deforestation occurs when lumber companies cut down all of the forests in a given area without replanting trees, although, currently, they are required to do so, by law. Another problem is that some corrupt timber magnates and Filipino politicians conspire in the illegal export of timber. Deforestation continues to be one of the major sources of ecological damage in the country, threatening all animal and plant species. Also, resource-rich marine mangroves and coral reefs are rapidly disappearing as a result of big commercial trawling, aquaculture, pollution, and illegal fishing practices that include the use of cyanides and dynamite to increase the catch.

The Philippine nation is part of Southeast Asia, encompassing Malaysia, Singapore, Brunei, and Indonesia. It has a strategic location and is open to different and diverse cultural influences coming from around Asia and beyond. Filipinos are mostly Malay people. The most significant ethnic minority is Chinese, and because of intermarriage, many Filipinos have Chinese ancestry. Also, the colonization of the islands by the Spanish (1565–1898) and Americans (1898–1946) has influenced the development of Philippine society and culture. There are some 78 different spoken languages and 500 dialects across the archipelago, all belonging to the Malayo-Polynesian linguistic family. While the majority of Filipinos can speak the national language—Tagalog, or Pilipino—and they share the same national identity, each different group tends to identify with the primary language group to which it belongs. The two principal languages are Tagalog, spoken in the provinces around Manila, and Cebuano, spoken throughout the Visayas and Mindanao. Other major languages are Ilocano, Hiligaynon, Bicol, Waray, Pampango, and Pangasinan. English is widely spoken throughout the islands and is the language of education and trade.

There are almost fifty other indigenous tribal groups in the Philippines, comprising about 20 percent of the population. They are historically and culturally different from the mainstream group of Filipinos and have long struggled to keep their land and cultural identity intact.

The Philippines is the only Christian nation in Asia. More than 60 percent of Asia's Christian population lives in the Philippines, and their numbers are increasing. In 1986 there were over 50 million Christians in the Philippines, and by the 1990s, this figure had reached over 65 million. There are approximately 11 million non-Catholic Christians practicing in over 350 organizations, most of which operate under the umbrella organization of the National Council of Churches in the Philippines. The largest denomination includes the gospel-style Philippines for Jesus movement and the Protestant Iglesia ni Cristo. The largest religious minority group is the Muslim population, with Islam being a much older presence than Christianity. Estimates of the Muslim population range between 3.9 million and 7 million, or 5 to 9 percent of the population. About 94 percent of these Filipino Muslims are concentrated in the western and southern part of the island of Mindanao, the Sulu archipelago, and in the southern tip of Palawan.[4]

Before the colonization of the Philippines by Spain and the United States, Filipinos were tolerant of other religions and did not discriminate among them. There was a significant amount of interreligious dialogue and exchange between the peoples of Asia in early times. The islanders were variously influenced by the spread of Hinduism, Buddhism, Daoism, Confucianism, and Islam throughout the region. However, the Spanish changed this dynamic as they brought with them the Roman Catholic Church, which was instrumental in setting up colonial rule over the islands. The close working relationship between the Roman Catholic Church and state, however, was dismantled by the U.S. colonial regime, which introduced a new religion, Protestant Christianity, and a new government mandate, the separation of church and state.

Today, religious freedom is guaranteed by the constitution. The contemporary disagreement between Muslim peoples of the southern islands and the federal government is not so much about religion as about political goals. However, the separation of church and state rule has never really been implemented in the Philippines. The Catholic Church still has a strong influence in some state legislation in the Philippines. The Catholic Church lobbied against the divorce law, which was not approved by the Congress and Senate. The Catholic and Protestant churches, too, have been influential in terms of democratization movements. They have organized people at the local levels for resistance, especially against Ferdinand Marcos's martial law dictatorship (1972–1986) and even now are speaking up for human rights.

POLITICS AND ECONOMY

The Philippine government is guided by the 1987 constitution, which provides for a presidential form of government. The president's term is limited, by law, to only six years. There are three branches of government: the executive presidency, the legislature, and the Supreme Court. Unlike the procedure followed in United States, the Philippine president selects all of the justices on the Supreme Court, without being subject to scrutiny and approval by the legislature. The bicameral legislature is comprised of 24 senators, who are popularly elected for a six-year term, and the House of Representatives consists of 220 congressmen (and congresswomen) who represent the local districts; 14 of the 220 representatives are party-list representatives.[5] Party-lists are organized lobby groups that represent the marginalized sectors of society. The president can select additional members of the lower house, up to the constitutionally mandated limit of 250 members. The president has considerable power over the legislature, as he or she controls the disbursement of appropriations. However, the actual power of the president is checked by the Congress, which oversees the national budget, officially proclaims the president and vice president, approves or disapproves promotions in the military, and conducts investigations on the performance of executive offices. The current president, Gloria Macapagal Arroyo (2001–), has had limited success in asserting her power over the executive branch of Congress. The power of the president can be greatly weakened by a fractious multiparty system, an ambitious and contentious Congress, and the lack of an adequate budget to fund programs that promote the commonwealth.

The contemporary Philippines has a liberal market economy that encourages privatization and free enterprise, with a large section in the hands of companies owned by a few wealthy families. Because these families control Congress, they have considerable influence over how government appropriations are allocated and used at the local levels. Filipinos have produced crops and mined minerals for export and sale on the world market for many years. Light-manufacturing industries produce textiles and electronics, machinery and transport equipment, coconut products, and chemicals. Almost one-quarter of exports go to the United States, while the remaining exports go to Japan and other Asian trading partners. With a population of approximately 82.4 million people as of 2004,[6] the Philippines has the highest population growth rate in Asia. Around 33.7 percent of this population is living below poverty. This population is growing and poses problems for policymakers seeking to solve the most pressing problems of poverty and environmental degradation.

The Philippines has a high literacy rate, widespread proficiency in English, as well as an educated workforce that has made Filipinos very competitive overseas. There were 988,615 Filipinos deployed to work overseas in more than 180 countries in 2005.[7] That same year, US$10,689,005 was remitted through banks alone.[8] Today, most Filipino families receive remittances from Filipinos working abroad.

The Philippines faces more difficult political and economic challenges ahead. Yet, the nation has succeeded in overcoming great obstacles in the past. It was one of the first countries to gain independence from colonial rule in 1946.

It was devastated by World War II (e.g., Manila was left in worse shape than Warsaw), but, by the 1960s, the nation emerged as a showcase for economic development and democratic government in the region. It had one of the highest literacy rates in Asia. However, the economy rapidly declined after President Ferdinand Marcos (1966–1986) declared martial law in 1972. Still, the democratic aspirations of the Filipino people did not subside, although for many years their free speech was suppressed and the people's movements continued underground. In 1986, they succeeded in ousting the dictator from office through a peaceful revolution. In 2001, a second People Power revolution was instrumental in helping to impeach President Joseph Estrada through parliamentary means. He was arrested on graft and corruption charges and found guilty by trial in court. Filipinos have long fought for the right to self-determination and self-government. If this book succeeds in presenting Philippine history in a way that is balanced and reflective of the Filipino struggle for democracy and freedom, then it will have achieved its purpose.

NOTES

1. *National Geographic Atlas of the World*, 6th ed. (Washington: National Geographic Society, 1992), p. 127.

2. Sonia Zaide, *A Unique Nation*, 2nd ed. (Quezon City: All Nations Publishing Co., 1999), pp. 8–9.

3. United Nations Food and Agricultural Organization, *The State of the World's Forests* (New York: UNFAO, 2003).

4. Eduardo Tadem, "The Political Economy of Mindanao: An Overview," in *Mindanao: Land of Unfulfilled Promise*, ed. Mark Turner, R. J. May, and Lulu Rospall Turner (Quezon City: New Day Publishers, 1992), p. 8.

5. *The Philippine Facts and Figures 2006* (Manila: National Statistics Office, 2006), p. 10.

6. This estimate based on a population count of the 2000 census (76.5 million) using a projected annual growth rate of 2.36 percent. http://www.census.gov.ph.

7. OFW Global Presence, *A Compendium of Overseas Employment Statistics 2005* (Manila: Philippine Overseas Employment Administration, 2005), p. 1.

8. OFW Global Presence, "Overseas Remittances by World Group 2004–2005," in *A Compendium of Overseas Employment Statistics 2005* (Manila: Philippine Overseas Employment Administration, 2005).

Timeline of Historical Events

3000 B.C.E.	Austronesian people begin arriving in the Philippines via Taiwan
500 B.C.E.	Philippine ports begin trading with China, Southeast Asia, and India
700 C.E.	Philippine trading intensifies under the Sri-Vijaya Empire (Indonesia)
1200s	Muslim (Arab and Persian) trading ports begin to form in Southeast Asia
1400s	Ming Chinese traders dominate the sea-lanes
1414	Prince Parameswara converts Mallaca into a great Muslim sea emporium
1450	Sayyid Abuy Bakhr establishes Sulu as a prominent center of Muslim trade and culture
1493	Pope Alexander VI issues Treaty of Tordesillas
1497	The Portuguese, under Vasco da Gama, reach West India

1521	Ferdinand Magellan arrives in the Philippines. King Lapu Lapu defeats Magellan, and his flotillas sail away
1557	The Portuguese capture Maccau and toll all Southeast Asian trade to the Arab coast
1565–1898	Spain colonizes the Philippines
1565	Miguel Lopez de Legazpi takes possession of Cebu
1571	Spain transfers its main navy base to Manila
1572	Manila becomes the center of Galleon Trade between Mexico and China
1577–1606	Franciscans, Jesuits, Dominicans, and Recollects enter the Philippines
1578	Spanish begin intermittent invasions of parts of Mindanao
1581	Bishop Salazar convenes first Catholic synod in Manila
1619–1671	Sultan Kudarat establishes formidable Maguindanao sultanate of Cotobato
1639	The Chinese revolt around Manila against conscript labor policy
1745	Rebellions break out in Bulacan, Batangas, Laguna, and Cavite
1762–1763	The British invade and occupy Manila
1763–1840	Chinese immigration to the Philippines is closed
1768	The Jesuits are ordered back to Spain. The archbishop of Manila supports the ordination of Filipino priests and transfer of parishes from missionary orders to diocesan orders
1872	Two hundred soldiers at Cavite revolt and call for independence. Fathers Gomez, Burgos, and Zamora are garroted to death for inspiring insurrection
1880s	Filipino Propaganda Movement gained ascendance
1888	*La Solidaridad* was founded by Graciano Lopez Jaena
1892	Jose Rizal founded the secret Liga Filipina order of the Propaganda Movement

1892	Andre Bonifacio initiates the Katipunan revolutionary movement
1896	Jose Rizal is accused of inciting rebellion and executed. General Emilio Aguinaldo replaces Bonifacio and leads the revolution
1896–1898	Filipino revolution for independence from Spanish colonialism
1897	Pact of Biak-na-Bato, a truce to cease fire. Revolutionary leadership goes into exile in Hong Kong
1898–1946	Colonization of the Philippines by the United States
1898	United States declares war on Spain. Commodore George Dewey allies with General Aguinaldo, who returns to the Philippines and declares independence. The United States signs the Paris Peace Treaty and purchases the Philippines from Spain for $20 million. President William McKinley proclaims "benevolent assimilation" and dispatches 70,000 troops to "pacify" the Philippines. The Filipino Revolutionary Congress declares and approves the First Republic and constitution with Aguinaldo as president
1900	Federalist Party launched by some 125 landed, elite Filipino collaborators
1901	President Aguinaldo is captured. President McKinley announces the end of the "insurrection." William Taft becomes the first civil governor. Major General Adna Chaffee succeeds General Arthur MacArthur and assigns Brigadier General Bell to conduct operations of terror in southern Luzon; General Smith's Samar campaign razes and massacres village populations
1902	General Miguel Malvar surrenders at Batangas, which officially ends the First Republic. Revolutionary guerilla operations commence underground. President Roosevelt officially announces the end of the war
1904	William Howard Taft recalled to the U.S. mainland to become secretary of war. Luke Wright becomes the new governor-general
1907	Elections first held for National Assembly. Nationalistas become dominant party. Sergio Osmena Sr. is elected

Speaker of the House, and Manuel Quezon elected majority floor leader

1909   U.S. Congress passes Payne Aldrich Bill (free-trade provision), and it is ratified by the Filipino assembly

1913   Francis B. Harrison becomes governor-general, until 1913, and implements the Filipinization policy

1916   President Wilson signs the Jones Law granting Philippine independence as soon as a stable government could be implemented. Philippine Commission is replaced by the Senate and House of Representatives

1921   President Harding dispatches Wood-Forbes Commission. General Leonard Wood, former military major general of Cuba and then the Muslim area of Mindanao, is appointed the new governor-general of the Philippines

1928   Henry Stimson succeeds Woods (deceased) as governor-general

1929   Dwight Davis is appointed the new governor-general

1933   President Roosevelt appoints pro-Independence advocate, Frank Murphy, as the new governor-general

1934   Tydings-McDuffe Act (Philippine Independence Act) enacted into law

1935   The new constitution is approved by President Franklin Roosevelt and the Filipino plebiscite. Quezon is elected president, and Osmenia vice president of the new commonwealth government

1936   Paul McNutt, who, unsuccessfully, argues against independence, becomes the new governor-general

1939   Francis Sayer of Harvard University and former secretary of state appointed new governor-general charged with preparing the Philippines for independence

1941   Quezon and Osmena are reelected, and the Philippine army is called into active service to fight against the Japanese invasion

1942   General Wainwright surrenders at Corregidor, which marks the end of the military's resistance, although guerilla units continue to resist the Japanese. Formation of Hukbong Bayan laban sa Hapon or Hukbalahap, also referred to as HUK (People's Army Against the Japanese)

1943   Japan-sponsored Second Republic of the Philippines is inaugurated with Jose Laurel as president

1944   President Quezon dies in New York. General Douglas MacArthur and his forces land on Leyte, with President Osmena, General Carlos Romulo, and General Basilio Valdez, who reinstate the commonwealth government

1945   General MacArthur transfers the powers of government to President Osmenia. Roxas splits from the Nationalistas and forms the Liberal Party

1946   The Philippine Congress approves the Bell Trade Act, which grants the United States parity rights and free rent for its military bases. Roxas defeats Osmena and declares the HUK and similar peasant organizations illegal Communist organizations

1948   President Roxas, who dies of a heart attack, is succeeded by his vice president, Quirino

1950   President Truman's Economic Survey Mission, also known as the Bell Commission, recommends rural reform, increasing production, and raising incomes. CIA Agent Lieutenant Colonel Edward Lansdale arrives to conduct counterinsurgency operations against the HUK. The armed forces of the Philippines (AFP) captures the top leadership of the Communist Party in Manila

1951   National Association for the Maintenance of Free Elections is established

1953   Magsaysay resigns from the Liberal Party to join the Nationalistas and is elected president

1954   The commander of the HUK forces, Luis Taruc, surrenders. Passage of the Agricultural Tenancy Act, which was established to deal with tenancy problems as well as to set up an agricultural credit and financing administration

1957   President Magsaysay dies in an airplane crash. Vice President Carlos Garcia is inducted into the office of president and wins the elections for another term

1958   President Garcia implements the Filipino First policy, which meets with opposition from the American, Chinese, and Chinese Filipino business communities

1960   International Rice Institute is established to develop new hybrid varieties of rice and corn with funding from the Ford Foundation and the Rockefeller Foundation

1961   Diosdado Macapagal is elected president and establishes the Program Implementation Agency to open up the economy

1963   Agricultural Land Reform Code passed by Congress, after they tack on some 200 amendments that protect their own personal assets

1965   Ferdinand Marcos changes his affiliation from the Liberal Party to the Nationalistas to run for office and is elected president. U.S. military bases in the Philippines become an important staging ground for the war in Vietnam

1968   Marcos launches military operations in Mindanao. Nur Misuari establishes the Moro National Liberation Front against the Marcos regime

1969   President Marcos and Vice President Lopez win a second term in office in a rigged election. The New People's Army, the armed branch of the Communist Party of the Philippines, is established

1971   Marcos stages several bombings, including the bombing of the Liberal Party rally held at Miranda Plaza, and accuses the Communists and suspends habeas corpus

1972   Marcos declares martial law and rounds up and arrests hundreds of critics, including Aquino and many others. Central Luzon is selected to test the Green Revolution, which aimed to increase production through hybrid varieties of rice and artificial inputs

1975   Aquino is brought before a military court and goes on a hunger strike

1977   Aquino is sentenced to death

1978   Marcos calls an election for an interim National Assembly. Jailed Aquino becomes the inspiration of the opposition that looses to Marcos's party (Kilusang Bagong Lipunan: New Society Movement)

1979   Aquino suffers a heart attack and is released from prison to undergo surgery in the United States

1981   Marcos lifts martial law and runs for reelection unopposed

1983   Aquino returns to the Philippines and is assassinated. His death inspires massive protests, and Cardinal Jamie Sin becomes more vocal in his criticism of the Marcos government

1984   Marcos suddenly calls for a "snap" presidential election. Cory Aquino declares her candidacy. The Communist Party calls for a boycott

1986   Marcos rigs the results and insists that he has won the election. A group of young officers organize RAM (Reform the Armed Forces Movement) and a coup. Marcos's forces, under General Ver, retaliate against them. Archbishop Sin mobilizes the massive People Power movement that surrounds and protects RAM. U.S. President Ronald Reagan scurries the Marcos family to Hawaii. Aquino assumes the presidency

1987   President Aquino establishes a revolutionary government under the Freedom Constitution. General Ramos quells several RAM-led coups; Aquino moves to the conservative right, reneging on campaign promises of change

1991   The Aquino administration passes the Local Government Code

1992   Fidel Ramos becomes the newly elected president. He appoints Vice President Estrada the chief of the Anti-Crime Commission. Kidnappings increase, especially of wealthy Chinese Filipinos

1993   President Ramos announces his Medium Term Development Plan to make the Philippines a developed country by the year 2000 and successfully breaks up some state-owned monopolies in telecommunications, shipping, and domestic airlines

1997   Asian economic crisis hits the Philippines

1998	President Ramos ends the International Monetary Fund's assistance; calls for a "Cha Cha" (charter change) to prolong his stay in office, which fails to gain support. Joseph Estrada becomes the new president
2000	The Abu Sayyaf Group abducts 23 teachers and 30 students in Basilan, and, after the cross fire between the government's soldiers and Abu Sayyaf terrorists, four hostages are found dead. Revelations of President Estrada taking payoffs from illegal gambling syndicates and national lottery funds, among other acts of malfeasance, lead to his impeachment trials, which are blocked by his allies in the Senate
2001	People Power II revolution demands Estrada's resignation. Gloria Arroyo Macapagal is declared vice president and sworn in by the Supreme Court as the new president. Abu Sayyaf kidnaps 16 people from a central Philippine resort, and AFP military officers are indicted and accused of helping the group escape in exchange for cash payment
2002	President Arroyo Macapagal supports U.S. President Bush's war on terror and deploys Philippine troops who, later, are assisted by the U.S. military in pursuit of Abu Sayyaf in Basilan
2004	President Arroyo Macapagal is elected to another six-year term. Opposition marches on the presidential palace, claiming election fraud
2005	President Arroyo Macapagal offers to submit herself to due process and stands trial before Congress. The parliamentary body formally rejects the motion by the opposition
2007	President Arroyo Macapagal's government continues to maintain political stability in the face of opposition

1

Southeast Asian Prehistory and the Philippines

Early Philippine history has to be viewed within the broader sweep of the history of Southeast Asia. Southeast Asia, of course, is a modern delineation and this region was contiguous with China in prehistoric times. However, Southeast Asia as defined here refers to the geographical area that includes the modern nation states of Vietnam, Burma, Laos, Cambodia, Thailand, Malaysia, Indonesia, and the Philippines. There are many unanswered questions when it comes to the study of precolonial settlements in the Philippines. Much of the early evidence of the coastal communities that probably existed and could have been used by modern archaeologists to learn more about these settlements was washed away when the seas rose, due to global warming, at the end of the last ice age, some 17,000 years ago. The warm and humid climate in the tropical zone has a disintegrating effect on bamboo and other plant-like materials that were used by the early inhabitants to build their homes, to make tools, and, later, for writing. Also, the many different ethnolinguistic and cultural groups have been unevenly studied by ethnographers. American archaeologists of the colonial era (1898–1946) tended to interpret their findings in terms of a continuous spread and overlay of human settlements that reached into the distant past. In the south, the Sunda Shelf connected the Philippines with the islands of Borneo, Java, and Sumatra, and with the entire peninsula of Malaysia and Vietnam, Thailand, and Cambodia. Northern Luzon was linked to Taiwan and formed the entry way to a broad land corridor leading into China. We now know that there were people in Java and China around the mid-Pleistocene, or during the ice age, some 300,000 years ago, as their remains along with stone implements and the bones of extinct animals have been found. Similar sites of stone tools and fossil remains, of large prehistoric animals, have been found in the Cagayan Valley of northern Luzon.

At the end of the ice age, when the seas began to rise again, the Philippines became an archipelago surrounded by water. It was already inhabited by small groups of hunters and gatherers who were self-supporting and self-sufficient. Around 7,000 years ago, food crops like rice and millet and a large number of legumes began to be developed in northeastern India, Burma, Thailand, and China, which is one of the earliest cradles of the Neolithic, or agricultural, revolution. Linguists have studied the movement of these migrating populations by tracing the spread of their language, Austronesian, which refers to a related group of languages spoken by the peoples of Indonesia, Malaysia, the Philippines, and Taiwan, as well as in parts of Vietnam. It is also the language of Polynesians found in the Micronesian islands, and some of the Melanesian groups. Some proto-Austronesian speakers carried the rice culture across the sea to northern Luzon, Philippines, from Taiwan, about 3000 B.C.E. Rice, basically, is a tropical and subtropical crop whose cultivation depends on water. Southeast Asia is in the monsoon zone and has soggy soil that is well suited for rice farming. There are two types of rice cultivation: Dry-rice cultivation, a form of shifting agriculture, involves planting rice on dry ground either by sowing in the wind or planting seeds in holes punched by digging sticks, after the existing vegetation has been cut. Wet-rice cultivation involves the use of germinated seeds that are planted in a seedbed. When these rice plants are about a foot high, they are transplanted. The plowing of the fields often is done with the help of a carabao, which is a much loved buffalo-like animal in the Philippines. Because wet-rice irrigation and planting involves a lot of cooperation between many groups of people, it expanded upon the earlier settlement patterns and increased the population.

Most of the descendents of the Malayo-Polynesians are seafarers, who carried their traditions through the entire expanse of the Pacific Ocean.[1] There are many hypotheses about the movement of peoples of the Pacific from the coast of south Asia, through the major archipelago of Southeast Asia in the western borders of the Pacific, in Neolithic times. Most of these theories are based on the existence of culture traits, or artifacts of material culture, that exhibit similar characteristics as reported from archaeological sites from these areas. The close relationship between the early peoples of the Philippines and Polynesia is demonstrated by the similarities in the types of stone tools and pottery used. Other similar artifacts made from shell have been found in profusion in the archaeological sites of Oceana. Domesticated plant and animal evidence, too, is conclusive. One of the oldest domesticated plants is the taro. The differentiation and distribution of this plant has been traced by archaeologist as moving from south Asia going north to Japan and south into New Caledonia, New Zealand, and Fiji. From Southeast Asia to Polynesia, there are only three domesticated animals: the dog, pig, and chicken. These animals are reported to have originated in Southeast Asia. Thus, the early Southeast Asian seafarers were highly skilled canoe builders and navigators who were able to sail clear across the Pacific, using their own bodily senses as their compass, at a time when almost all of the Europeans thought such travel was impossible.

Sometime in the last 2,000 years, we can see archaeological and linguistic evidence for the existence of a world maritime trade economy that was similar to that of the Mediterranean, only much larger in scale, and that connected the Philippines to China, India, and the Arab and Persian lands. Hindu, Buddhist, Taoist, and Confucian influences were, creatively, absorbed and transformed in the Philippines through an interactive process of adoption and adaptation. About 1200 C.E., Islam began to spread to Southeast Asia, as some sultanates also developed in the Philippines, especially southern Mindanao.

TRADE AND THE RISE OF LOCAL RULERS

The warm and tropical monsoon winds, blowing from the northeast in northern winter, and the southeast during the northern summer, contributed to the development of a prosperous and growing regional trade economy. Since these winds regularly reversed direction every season, the early Southeast Asians learned to plan their seafaring journeys in accordance with the changing winds. They could sail with relative ease across a big expanse of ocean to visit trading partners and relatives and then, after resting a while, ride home with the wind. The relative ease and safety with which people could travel encouraged increases in material and cultural exchanges. Also, the tropically rich vegetative cover and, usually, congenial topography of the islands made it relatively comfortable to walk on foot or sail. There are so many islands around the archipelago interconnected by landfills and waterways with well-sheltered bays and protected harbors. Trade over land and sea brought new people in contact with one another, ranging from upland hunters and gatherers and horticulturalists to the complex chiefdoms and states of south and Southeast Asia and northeast Asia.

Maritime trade encouraged widespread social, cultural, and economic changes throughout the region. It introduced new people with different religious and political backgrounds who helped to shape, as they were shaped by, the development of local histories and hierarchies. The geographical boundaries between these communities or, more accurately, mandalas, were porous and fluid; foreigners could be transformed into friends, or even family if they married, through engaging in trade or an apprenticeship relation to share sacred knowledge. New leaders could arise who recognized a potentially powerful trade partner who promised to bring in prestige goods. These rulers sometimes took Indic titles like rajah, derived from Sanskrit, to distinguish their descendents as members of a royal lineage. They traded in valuable heirlooms such as legendary swords, icons, and relics that were accorded a spiritual essence that filled them and their people with sacred power. However, it is important to note that although rajahs could pass down their titles and wealth to their children, they could easily be usurped from power when stronger leaders emerged. Thus, the office of rajah or chief could be either inherited or achieved through competition in early Philippine society.

Kinship still played an integral and important role in the development of local hierarchies.[2] Unlike in northeast Asia (China, Korea, and Japan), a large and impersonal state bureaucracy never developed in the Philippines. Instead, there were numerous competing centers of power whose rulers strove not to colonize their neighbors but to include them in their networks of kith and kin. Communities of relatives and friends developed as children grew up and married, building their homes adjacent to parents on either side of the family. The boundaries separating these communities were in a state of fluidity and shifted as new alliances were formed, histories coalesced, and new leaders emerged.

Local leaders were distinctive because they had an ability to entice followers who cooperated in religious and scholarly, ritual, agricultural, commercial, and military matters. Such leaders replaced or incorporated the previous ancestral line of the community into their own by achieving the title of village ancestor. They were able to cultivate followers by engaging in reciprocal exchanges. They were believed to have divine spiritual energy that enabled them to keep social relations within and between communities, and between the earth and the cosmos, in balance. Social confusion resulting from a rupture in the network of reciprocity and exchange, or chaos occurring in times of natural calamity, was indicative of a ruler's decline, at which point people moved to follow a new authority.

In Southeast Asia, personal power was perceived by the local people differently than in the Western worldview. That is, power was not an abstraction as it is in Western social thought, but, rather, it is an existential reality.[3] There were indigenous signs that indicated a powerful ruler. A powerful leader was perceived to be pure "not in a moralistic sense but rather in terms of his or her ability to concentrate and diffuse power." That is, there was a "direct relation between a person's inner self and their capacity to control the environment."[4] Also, there were apparent signs of a leader; one had "radiance" about them, one was sexually fertile, and one surrounded oneself with sacred objects and people who held unusual power so as to absorb it vicariously. Leaders wore and distributed "magic" amulets, uttered formulaic prayers, and believed that their weapons, and personages, were invincible in times of battle.[5] Conversely, defeat in battle or the diminishment of a ruler's wealth and following was perceived by local people to be a sign of a leader's dwindling inner strength.

In other words, the projection and recognition of charismatic leadership and authority around the Philippine archipelago was a local matter. Social transformations occurred as foreign influences were selectively reinvented, and they were specific to the conventions of a particular community.

INDIC AND CHINESE INFLUENCES

Some of the earliest known influences came from Hindu and Buddhist traders and monks who exchanged textiles and other sacred gifts for local and Chinese wares. They introduced new religious rituals and political forms of behavior. However, this should not be mistaken to mean that the inhabitants of the Philippine islands blindly accepted the Hindu belief system and way of life. Rather, they selectively integrated what they perceived to be useful Hindu notions into their already existing animistic beliefs and practices. Early local rulers adopted Hindu titles, like rajah, and accompanying accouterments to enhance their spiritual and political power. The term *Visaya* (*Vijaya*), which refers to the central group of islands in the Philippines, is suggestive of her place in the Hindu tributary system. There are few known Hindu artifacts, such as the 1,790 gram, 21 karat gold Hindu goddess of Agusan, which is on display in the Chicago Natural History Museum.[6] One probable explanation for the scarcity of ancient Hindu, Buddhist, or shamanistic scripts and material remains is due to the Spanish colonizers having destroyed pagan icons and books in their wake. Unlike in Bali, Indonesia, Hindu temple complexes were never built in stone in the ancient Philippines. However, there is substantial archaeological and historical evidence pointing to the existence of many small trading centers that specialized in the production of prestige goods (e.g., potteries, textiles, medicinal plants, and decorative plumes) for trade and exchange as tribute.

One of the earliest known maritime Southeast Asian states to do business with traders in the Philippines was the Sri-Vijaya Empire coming out of Indonesia, which controlled east–west trade through the Straight of Malacca for 400 years from 700 to 1100 C.E.[7] Sri-Vijaya was strategically located not far from the southern Philippines, at the southern most tip of Sumatra, inland along the Musi River, which flows out into the Malacca Straight, at the very crossroads of sea trade. It had a powerful navy that punished pirates and protected foreign ships by allowing them safe passage through the straights. It grew to become one of the most important clearinghouse centers for exchange and export to the west. The river provided inhabitants with access to a wide variety of products and offered them a safe and secure harbor. At first, this community was self-sufficient in food production. However, over time, the population multiplied and expanded its territory further upriver to the coasts. The Sri-Vijayas formed a pact with the Javanese, who then supplied them with rice. Although these two communities did not always agree with each other and sometimes even fought, mostly, they prospered together in peace and harmony through marriage and trade alliances.

The Sri-Vijaya Empire began to decline in the 1400s, when the Chinese came to dominate Southeast Asian sea trade.[8] There was a sudden increase in the population during the Ming dynasty (1368–1644 C.E.) that in combination with the frequent outbreaks of infectious diseases such as the measles and small pox epidemics of 1407, 1410, 1411, and 1413, probably further instigated the Chinese to search for additional sources of supplies, especially medicinal herbs. Famous mariners, like General Zheng He, who commandeered the emperor's fleet of 48 treasure ships in 1409, began to develop an elaborate set of tributary networks through the use of diplomacy; force, if needed; and the giving of tribute to local rulers, who, in turn, acknowledged China's supremacy. Local ambassadors and dignitaries were escorted back with the tribute missions to pay homage to the Chinese emperor. They were treated with great hospitality and accorded the full dignity and splendor of their rank and title. Only local rulers who were recognized by the Chinese emperor were allowed to participate in its expanding network of trade and exchange, and thus local and competing Philippine leaders could build up their own power and notoriety in relation to their place in the celestial order of the Middle Kingdom.

THE COMING OF ISLAM

Islam was transmitted to Sumatra and Java by Arab and Persian traders and missionaries in the thirteenth century, although earlier Muslim trading sites existed in the region. As Islam began to spread rapidly after the death of the Prophet Muhammad in 632, Arabia emerged as one of the important centers of commerce and culture. Arab and other Muslim traders and sailors were the intermediaries between Asian merchants and European traders.[9] As these Muslims converted local rulers and their retainers, their trade networks also expanded. One of the earliest rulers to convert to Islam was the banished prince of Palembang origin, Parameswara, who ran away from the Javanese court to settle in a small fishing village on the island of Malacca. In 1405, he swore his allegiance to the Chinese emperor, for which he was rewarded a seal of investiture recognizing Malacca as an independent kingdom. Parameswara's maneuver infuriated the Javanese and Siamese; the latter royal courts claimed the island was their territory, but they felt helpless to do anything about it for fear of antagonizing the powerful Chinese. Soon after, Malacca became a favorite stopover for Muslim traders to sit out the long monsoon season. In 1414, they encouraged the prince to adopt Islam and form a marriage alliance with one of the Muslim princesses of Pasai. Malacca soon went on to become one of the greatest sea emporiums in Southeast Asia, overshadowing neighboring ports. The courtly demeanors and court language, Malay, that once served as the language of trade and communication throughout much of Southeast Asia, began to be replaced by Arabic, as Arabic beliefs and practices gained in ascendance. However, the Vijayan courtly demeanor based on loyalty, marriage alliances, and trade never really went away but remained alongside newer Islamic forms.

One of the earliest sultanates to develop, thereafter, in the Philippines was on the Sulu island chain, off the coast of Borneo. Islam was introduced there by early Chinese traders and Muslim missionaries during the Ming dynasty in the fourteenth century. However, it wasn't until 1450, when the Sumatran sultan, Sayyid[10] Abu Bakhr, married a local princess that Sulu became a prominent center of Muslim trade and culture. Rulers living across the sea on Mindanao, and elsewhere in the Philippines, soon realized that they could benefit by participating in the growing Muslim trade networks. They could gain more wealth and, thereby, further solidify their power by surrounding themselves with larger armies and slaves, which strengthened their ability to collect tribute and build new alliances. Although Muslim rulers believed that all were equal in the eyes of one God and did not believe in slavery, only debt bondage, and freed slaves once converted, they still believed they could capture and enslave non-Muslims. While this created a new dichotomy between Muslims and non-Muslims, the division between slaves and masters existed long before the arrival of Islam in Southeast Asia.

ANCIENT ASIAN SLAVERY SYSTEMS

Diverse religious and philosophical traditions exerted some influence over the formation of different slavery systems pertaining to Southeast Asia. While the institutionalization of slavery may have nothing to do with Buddhism and Confucianism as envisioned by the founders, Buddha and Confucius, Confucianism and Buddhism still advocated a specific social order of hierarchy, namely, that of serving the king. While Buddhism diverged from Hinduism, it continued to be informed by Hindu cultural ideas and practices. The Buddhist occupation with merit making and harmonious coexistence with all life-forms, coupled with Hindu notions of caste and hierarchy, coalesced with the open system of slavery as practiced in ancient Thailand. In comparison, the Chinese Confucian interest in following lines of authority through kinship that ranked people according to age level, and that placed ancestors over the living, seniors over juniors, males over females, and male scholars over commoners, fit nicely with the closed system of slavery in ancient Vietnam. Hinduism, Buddhism, and Chinese Confucianism provided some influence over the development of the different Southeast Asian systems of slavery. This was the case in the precolonial Philippines, where a mixture of Hindu/Buddhist, Confucian, and, later, Islamic notions were selectively integrated into already existing systems of debt bondage. A basic understanding of the distinctive differences between Buddhism and Confucianism, as illustrated by way of ancient Thailand and China,[11] is important to understanding this chapter's closing discussion on the early Philippine system that predated and existed in contradistinction to Spanish colonial Christianity.

THAI BUDDHIST SLAVERY

Thai history has long been informed by Buddhist and Hindu social teachings. Unlike in India or China, where genealogical links are largely traced through the male lines, in Thailand, genealogies are traced bilaterally through both the male and female side of the family. It is Thai daughters, not sons, who are expected to take care of their parents when they get old. This horizontal status accorded to both sexes is offset in so far as Thai females always were considered property either of their father's household or husband's household. Female slaves were definitively valued for their contribution to sexual reproduction and as second wives and concubines, although a father or husband who sold his daughter or wife into bondage in times of starvation or financial hardship in former times could keep her at home as long as he paid the interest on the loan. Moreover, a free person, formerly, had to substantially demonstrate that he was over his head in debt and desperately poor before he could legally sell any member of his household, or himself, into slavery, or he would be severely punished according to law. Buddhism, as well, mitigated some of the harsher effects of slavery, as it was viewed as meritorious, and slaves had some rights against owners who transgressed the boundaries of their sexual rights. Slaves, also, could possess private property, and some of them were entrusted in positions of authority over other slaves and free clients.

Historically, Thais practiced an open-ended form of slavery that was theologically oriented around Buddhist ideas of a galactic order, and even the king of Siam was said to be a slave of Buddha. Much like India, Thailand has a philosophy of a coming of a just and righteous king. In times of judicious and benevolent kingship, social life is said to be replete with a bountiful harvest and harmonious relationships that produce a popular feeling of well-being. Duplicitous, selfish kingships, conversely, mark times of bad harvest and social disruption. The ancient system of slavery in Thailand, not unlike that in precolonial Philippines, albeit in different guise, was really a form of debt slavery; men and women could "buy" their freedom. There were laws in place that guaranteed basic rights.[12] Free clients and slaves often were perceived to be living on the same level in terms of status, and sometimes, slaves (e.g., temple slaves) held substantially higher stations than those who were free of bondage. The king held most slaves and divided them between princes (and leading monks) in exchange for their loyal service in governing the kingdom. Slaves were a symbol of luxury and wealth, but Thai society was not oriented around slavery as an economic system, because slaves worked alongside free clients. Typically, freemen and their families were self-sufficient subsistence farmers who worked the king's land and who could be called, within reasonable guidelines, by royal administrators to provide food and to labor on construction projects for the kingdom.

The Thai system of slavery might be called more "feudal" in nature. The slave had many of the same modes of entry into slavery that were found in China, that of conquest, war, capture, and being "sold," but there is the added aspect of the debt slave, who may or may not be redeemable. By redeemable, it is meant that one's debts might eventually either be worked off or paid off and the condition of slavery diminished and the slave freed. In addition, there are other forms of slavery not commonly found in China, for example, that of judicial or temple slaves. The temple slaves were on occasion those who placed themselves into service, since in some cases the life of the temple slave might be viewed as actually better than the life of the freed person. They were exempt from mandatory labor requirements, and those services they did provide were lighter than other forms of slavery. Regarding slaves of war and conquest, for example, many tens of thousands were taken by the Siamese in the wars against the Khmer Empire in the fourteenth century.[13] These were by far the most common since there were many reasons that population numbers might become so low that only an outside infusion of bodies could maintain the community. Frequent warfare was a form of competition for a loyal following, not territory, and no doubt helped to reproduce the local population, which was often ravaged and depleted by the spread of diseases such as malaria and small pox, famines, floods, droughts, and raids. These slaves were then redistributed among nobles, according to their rank, while some were donated to temple services. Sometimes, the latter slaves were commissioned by the king to build new temples in distant and remote regions, to win the local community's support and loyalty.

In addition, slaves served another function, as a form of exchange and tribute. So the use of slaves became more than the acquisition of a labor force and a replacement population, but a political and economic exchange used to pay off debts and influence the political atmosphere. Thai slaves were mainly absorbed and absolved, rather than freed or made kin. While the entire subject is more complicated, there is enough groundwork here to distinguish the Thai system of slavery from the Euro-colonial type. We now turn to a discussion on the ancient Chinese and, then, Philippine systems of slavery.

EARLY CHINESE SLAVERY

China has been long influenced by Confucian social teachings. Unlike in Thailand, where the family tree is traced bilaterally through the male and female lines, in China, genealogical links are recorded over the generations through male ties. Chinese females are perceived to be outsiders. They are never named in ancestral rites, and their primary role is to bear male heirs. A female could enter into domestic household service as a maid or child servant, and, in that case, she might be adopted as a younger sister and become part of the family. Alternatively, she would be arranged into an exogamous marriage, sometimes as a child bride. While the bride-price for the first wife was high, it was transformed into a dowry, and the marriage rite itself marked the transference of certain rights and privileges to her. In contrast, the primary role of second wives was to produce sons, while concubinage was for pleasure. Matchmakers arranged the sale of maids, brides, concubines, and prostitutes, privately, out of the public view.

Slaves in ancient China found themselves in a closed system. As a rule, slaves in China were born as slaves or purchased as children, in addition to the purchase of concubines by the wealthy. While the potential for slaves to alter or change their status was open in Thailand, that opportunity was extremely limited in China, yet not completely absent. China is a strictly patriarchal society, and as such, any inclusion of males into the lineage would constitute a threat to existing heirs, since this would cause further division of property at the death of the clan head. Therefore, males who were not purchased as children for replacement heirs (meaning there were no other heirs) were suspended in permanent slave status, although eunuchs were accorded high status because they were believed to be more loyal and powerful (e.g., they usually served the emperors royal court). Watson explains that girls had more freedom than boys did once they became slaves, for the boys would enter their new life either as an heir or lifelong servant. Females had more tangible opportunities for improving their situation through marriage.[14] Chinese women were considered as belonging to, rather than being in, the kinship line, even when they married within it. Since they did not have any inheritance rights that would have been recognized or supported, they were not considered a threat and, therefore, had more social mobility than men did.

China created its own supply of slaves from within by creating stratification within its own social structure; taking its slaves from within that created a "lower" class. The stigma attached to the status of a slave did not only last a lifetime, but for subsequent generations of slaves. This can be traced back to the Chinese practice of ancestor worship. The Chinese viewed belonging to a lineage as a requirement for being considered a civilized person. Since the males were carriers of the lineage, even the poorest farmers would resist selling their sons until all the daughters and even the wife were sold. For example, they would sell their sons to save them from dying from starvation. This attitude resulted in fewer males on the market, and thus males demanded higher prices. This practice repeatedly disrupted the male slaves' ancestral lines, so that the slaves, in essence, never developed a family line and their hereditary relatives remained unknown. In some modern cases, the ancestral line might be invented in an effort to conceal lack of ancestry. Once a slave was purchased, there would be some expense on the part of the master. Feeding, clothing, and housing the slave might become overly burdensome, especially if the master took on a significant number of slaves. The slave market, with these financial concerns and with an abundance of slaves for sale, in effect, created what we today call a buyer's market. Within this market, the largest portion of slaves were females; however, females could loose their slave background through marriage, while male slaves and their male offspring were stigmatized for many generations to come.

Hence, Chinese male slaves, unless adopted as heirs, were locked into a closed system of slavery, while female slaves could marry their way out. However, this slave market system based on use value, not exchange value, was transformed when the European colonizers came to China. The Europeans brought and introduced their habit of buying and selling slaves as if they were only material objects, which was an affront and contrary to ancient Asian codes, in general, that provided slaves with certain rights and social security.

ANCIENT PHILIPPINE SLAVERY

The Philippines experienced a mélange of religious and philosophical influences prior to the colonial period. Underlying Hindu, Buddhist, and Islamic faiths were widespread and intermingled with indigenous beliefs and practices that were informed by animistic nature "worship." The economy was engaged in a maritime trade economy that extended far beyond Southeast Asia. Local communities were dispersed along estuaries of rivers and coastal shores, each settlement scattered to protect the residents from the possibility of offshore slave raiders. Each community's individual history was made up of a complex of local histories wherein leaders were legitimated by their followers, in relation to even wider concentric networks, or mandalas, of power. Chiefdoms existed, in that the office of chief was ordinarily inherited and there was a redistributive system wherein slavery was a key component. However, as a check on their authority, the office of chief (rajah or *datu*) was also achieved, and the center of redistribution shifted as new leaders emerged.

The system of slavery in the Philippines was a far-reaching and complex system that differed dramatically from, and existed in utter contradistinction to, the Euro-American transatlantic slave trade system.[15] In contrast to the European colonial system where slaves were supplied in the market, slaves in the Philippines often shared the same ethnicity, language, and descent as their masters. Parents frequently arranged the marriage of their young children by turning over a number of slaves in good faith. Men often sold themselves into slavery to their fathers-in-law as a form of bride-price, much in the same way as Jacob did for the hand of Rachel and Leah, as told in the Christian Bible.[16] Almost everyone was indebted to someone else to some degree, and slavery in this sense was endemic. Slaves, generally, took a good deal of satisfaction in being attached to their masters. The various types of slaves ranged from those captured for ransom in raids at one extreme to those who sold themselves into slavery to someone for whom they felt a debt of gratitude from the heart at the other extreme. While some slaves were sacrificed, for example, in times when a boat was launched or when a great seafarer had passed away, most slaves lived ordinary lives not much different from those who were free. Except for slaves living inside their master's house, slaves were expected to support themselves, working part time for their owners, while the owners themselves were usually enslaved to other masters.[17]

Kinship played an important role in the development of debt bondage on the islands. Family networks and lineages were traced bilaterally through both the female and male lines. This diminished the importance of status based on lineage connections to a single female or male ancestor. Instead, important genealogical claims were based on achieving a founding line of descent and establishing fictive kin relations horizontally in the present. This emphasis on the present had an impact on how the master–slave bond emerged locally, where social relations, not private property, were highly valued. Customary interactions between masters and slaves in this context were mutually respectful.

The coming of the Spanish colonizers to the Philippines with their different habits and worldview was an affront to the cultural ethos and common sense of mutual well-being. Spanish colonial processes profoundly and irreversibly disrupted and altered local practices, and the effect of this influence should not be underestimated. However, local motifs and customary forms of behavior continued to reemerge in new guises and resisted the colonial design.

NOTES

1. For a detailed account of the prehistoric voyages of the Malayo-Polynesians, see Peter Bellwood, "The Austronesian Dispersal and the Origin of Languages," *Scientific American*, Vol. 265, No. 1 (July 1991), pp. 88–93.

2. Vincent Rafael, *Contracting Colonialism: Translation in Christian Conversion in Tagalog Society under Early Spanish Rule* (Ithaca: Cornell University Press, 1988), p. 13.

3. Reynaldo Ileto, *Pasyon and Revolution: Popular Movements in the Philippines, 1840–1910* (Quezon City: Ateneo de Manila Press, 1979), pp. 30–31.

4. Reynaldo Ileto, *Pasyon and Revolution*, p. 31.

5. Anthony Reid, *Slavery, Bondage, and Dependency in Southeast Asia* (New York: St. Martin's Press, 1983), p. 7.

6. Sonia Zaide, *Butuan, The First Kingdom* (Butuan City: Artop Printing House, 1990), p. 42.

7. Patricio Abinales and Donna Amoroso, *State and Society in the Philippines* (New York: Rowan and Littlefield, 2005), chap. 2.

8. Louise Levathes, *When China Ruled the Seas* (Oxford: Oxford University Press, 1994).

9. Majul, Cesar Adib, *Muslims in the Philippines* (Quezon City: University of the Philippines Press, Diliman, 1999), p. 41.

10. *Sayyid* signifies descent from the Prophet Muhammad.

11. James Watson, "Transactions in People: The Chinese Market in Slaves, Servants, and Heirs," in *Asian and African Systems of Slavery*, ed. James L. Watson (Berkeley: University of California Press, 1980), pp. 223–250.

12. Andrew Turton, "Thai Institution of Slavery," in *Asian and African Systems of Slavery*, ed. James Watson, p. 251–292.

13. Andrew Turton, "Thai Institution of Slavery," in *Asian and African Systems of Slavery*, ed. James Watson, p. 256.

14. James Watson, "Transactions in People: The Chinese Market in Slaves, Servants, and Heirs," in *Asian and African Systems of Slavery*, ed. James Watson, p. 224.

15. Kathleen Nadeau, "Prostitutes and Slavery in Asia: Does the Market Set the Captives Free?" *Critical Asian Studies*, Vol. 34, No. 1 (2002), pp. 149–159.

16. *Christian Community Bible* (Philippines: Claretian Publications, 1991), Genesis 29.

17. William Henry Scott, *Slavery in the Spanish Philippines* (Manila: De La Salle University Press, 1982).

2

Spanish Colonization (1521–1896)

The Spanish colonization of the Philippines was a significant historical event in the sixteenth century. However, colonization was never so central a phenomenon as to outweigh in importance local historical developments that were already long in place. Some strong Muslim states were well established in the archipelago toward the end of the fifteenth century in Sulu and Magindanao in southern Mindanao and Manila on northern Luzon. In the region, China, Korea, and Japan held economic and political sway. Colonization and Christianization forcibly changed the course of development of Philippine history. However, Spain was never able to suppress long-established cultural patterns. This chapter examines the historical processes that underpinned the Spanish colonization of the Philippines. It brings into consideration local viewpoints and ways of life that existed in contradistinction to the European framework. It is by looking at this complex interplay between these two different and opposing systems that we can begin to see some of the factors that helped to shape the modern Philippine nation-state.

THE PHILIPPINES IN THE SIXTEENTH CENTURY

At the coming of the Spaniards, there were an estimated 500,000 people living in the Philippines.[1] They comprised a large number of distinctly different cultural and linguistic groups of which most were lineal descendants of Malay immigrants who came to the Philippines from south and Southeast Asia. They lived on the coasts and along inland bays and rivers. Much of the information that we now have about sixteenth-century Philippine society comes from early chronicles recorded by Spanish clerics. These texts have been closely examined by William Henry Scott (1921–1993), the distinguished American historian who made his home, after World War II, in the Philippines. He wrote many books about the different societies and cultures of the Philippines at the time of the Spanish arrival. During the sixteenth century, some of the colonial friars learned to speak the local languages in order to better convert and control the Filipinos. They compiled dictionaries filled with details of everyday life, especially in the Cebuano- and Tagalog-speaking regions. However, their versions of history need to be reread carefully with critical discernment because they were written from an ethnocentric perspective. Also, these entries were spread out over chronological time and geographical space, so they contain conflicting information that is fragmented because of the slowness of Spanish colonization. However, we can still find in these well-illustrated texts a window onto the ancient past.

We can see in the sixteenth-century descriptions of the different societies and cultures and how they were organized. Most of the different communities shared in common a three-tier caste system. The term *caste* is used here interchangeably with *class* to define different types of work in relation to a dynamic hierarchical structure, and it is not to be confused with the more rigidly arranged south Indian caste system in ancient times. There were three main classes: the rulers, commoners, and slaves. Rulers were the overseers of *barangays,* or small political units. The word *barangay* has two etymological root words—boat and a small political unit—and is indicative of the dependence people had on their boats in every day life. The word *barangay* was adopted by the Visayans from the Tagalogs after the Spanish arrived, when Manila became the capital. Rulers distributed community property and passed down final judgments in legal proceedings. Usually, *datus,* called *datos* in Spanish, were great warriors because their primary responsibility was to defend their *barangays* from outsiders. Among the Visayans, *datus* corresponded to noble princes and princesses, *timawas* were the ordinary citizens, and the *oripun* were slaves. The Visayans considered their class system to be so important that they divided the animal kingdom according to it. Little green parrots and green ones with red breasts were *timawas,* while those with resplendent red and green plumage were *datus.*[2] According to the Visayan origin myth,[3] the three primary classes corresponded to the original offspring of a primordial couple who were running away from their father's wrath. Depending on where they hid in his house, they were accorded a special class status. The ancient Visayans, not unlike the Balinese,[4] divided the spatial orientation of their homes along three lines: the inner rooms were for nobles; the outer rooms, for ordinary citizens; and the kitchen and in-between the walls, for slaves. All others who went out of the house were traveling ambassadors.

Among the Muslim Tagalogs, the office of *datu* was inherited and passed through the male line due to the male-centered influence of Islam, but the power of office depended on the loyalty of commoners and slaves who could give their allegiance to the *datu* of their choice. While the Tagalog rulers proba-bly were more merchant-like than warlike, they also organized and conducted raids, avenged grievances, waged vendettas, seized captives, and took human lives in mourning for other prominent chiefs. The Tagalogs fought with the usual Philippine weapons: the single-edged dagger, the wavy kris, spears with both metal and fire-hardened tips, padded armor and carabao-hide breast plates, and long narrow shields. The bow and arrow was used only in certain regions, and the blowgun nowhere. Those with access to foreign imports some-times had Japanese swords or Chinese peaked helmets.[5]

The early Tagalogs' conceptions of a *datu*'s power were informed by the teachings of mystical Islam, which was underlain by Hindu and Shaman be-liefs. They carried their religion with them from Indonesia, Malaysia, and Bor-neo. Perhaps this is why the Spaniards who first encountered them considered the Tagalogs only vaguely Muslim.[6] Nonetheless, their understanding of a *datu*'s power was based on a disciple-to-master relationship, which Shaman-ism, Hinduism, and Islam held in common.

Tagalog commoners, or *timawa*, were literally free persons. They were usu-ally prohibited from marrying into the *datu* class. The only possible exceptions to this rule would be during periods of instability and political realignment within a community that moved to anoint a new *datu* from outside the village, or *datu* class, in which case their family was fitted into the genealogy of the collective as ancestor. Many commoners were illegitimate children of the aris-tocracy, while others were formerly slaves who had earned their new status. Commoners entered into contractual relations with *datus* who awarded them portions of the *barangay* land to farm and pass on without being subject to trib-ute. In return, they joined their leader as partners on fishing and raiding expe-ditions, at harvest time, and in other enterprises. The commoners could expect generous shares of the *datu*'s bounty for exceptional performance. Their free status depended on their ability to indebt others and to avoid being indebted themselves.

The *alipin* class included two categories of slaves known as the *namamahay* and *gigilid*. Members of this class were commoners who incurred a debt, off-spring who inherited the debt of their parents, and prisoners or captives of war. The *namamahay* were analogous to tribute payers. They acquired a right to a piece of land and were obligated to return a portion of the harvest to their masters. In addition, they worked as needed for their master in other capacities such as building houses or serving as oarsmen on excursions. They were often rewarded for their services, and they could use their savings to purchase their freedom.

The *gigilid* were members of the slave class who lived under the same roof as their master or in the home of a commoner to whom they were indebted. As household helpers, they were commonly treated like members of the family. However, if they were captive slaves, they were treated more like property. Typically, *gigilid* acquired *namamahay* status once married, as they were given a separate house and a piece of land to work. Like *namamahay*, they could work off their debts and obtain status as free persons.

In practice, the social and political hierarchy of the Tagalogs had built-in opportunities for social mobility. Members of the elite gained their enhanced statuses by entering into a circle of relationships of varying degrees of reciprocity and indebtedness, wherein rulers were the last to be indebted. Local leaders were connected to their followers, and they were the ones who made sure that all surplus was circulated back into the community, even as it was exchanged in the wider Asian maritime economy. Leaders, generally, lost the allegiance of their followers if they were unable to oversee the commonwealth or if they betrayed the public trust. People represented the greatest resource for local elites because the human community brought into being both the products and protective measures leaders needed to maintain their political power. They were not protected by a large outside apparatus of state.

However, Spanish colonization (1521–1896) changed the social structure of Philippine society. The Spaniards used a strategy to colonize the islands that was similar to the one they used to colonize the New World.[7] They preserved local leaders who collaborated with them to convert their following and used them to exploit their own people and the environment. However, typical authority positions in the New World (e.g., the Aztec civilization and the Maya kingdom) as part of a state apparatus were inherited. By contrast, Filipino leadership positions were open and contestable, even when inherited, because they were part of autonomous communities. The Spaniards undermined this traditional authority system because they governed by use of military force and solidified in office crony chiefs, who were obeyed but often lost the respect of their own people. The Europeans were driven by their desire for wealth and profit. They wanted to dominate and control the spice trade that stretched from this part of the world to the European markets. This is the subject of the next section.

SIXTEENTH-CENTURY EUROPE AND ASIA

The Philippines at the time when the Spanish arrived was part of an ancient Asian civilization with a long and glorious history. Asians traded in silk and cotton textiles when medieval Europeans were still exchanging animal skins for coarsely spun materials. Asians had already achieved far greater advances in seamanship, science, medicine, civil administration, and foreign diplomacy than had medieval Western Europeans.[8] Asian societies and cultures were prospering, and their people enjoyed a much higher standard of living than did Europeans. By the sixteenth century, when the Spaniards first came to the Philippine islands, the local people were trading not only with each other but with neighboring countries like China, Japan, Korea, India, Arabia, Siam, Cambodia, Java, Brunei, Malacca, Borneo, Celebes, and the Moluccas. Foreigners brought silks, precious porcelains, iron implements and tools, and other products to the Philippines, in exchange for gold, pearls, resins, medicinal herbs, beeswax, rattans, exotic flowers, various kinds of woods and other rich forest and sea products, and textiles and other handicrafts.

Before the colonial conquest, Filipinos were engaged in tributary relationships that diplomatically interconnected the different cultures and societies of the Asian region and beyond. Lowlanders were involved in mutually beneficial trade relations with upland hunters and gatherers and horticulturalists to obtain rare goods for home use or trade in the wider economy. The indigenous communities had their own systems of governance and economy that differed starkly from that of the colonizers. Mostly traders, sea merchants, fish harvesters, cultivators, and craftspeople lived in small, integrated communities with production based on use value as opposed to exchange value. Surplus was produced, but only in the sense of an excess of goods normally used for consumption set aside for appropriation and circulation.

Goods produced in Asia made their way to ancient Europe, mainly by way of three trade routes: The famous Silk Road that crossed central Asia to the Black Sea; from there the goods went mainly to Constantinople but also found their way into Europe up the Danube River. Spices exchanged in Ceylon went to the Persian Gulf and then up to Baghdad and over to Syrian coastal towns along the Mediterranean Sea. This latter route of trade was most widely used, up until the time of the Crusader invasion, and, most especially, before Baghdad was destroyed by the Mongols in 1258. From then on, a third route of trade was taken across the Indian Ocean and through the Red Sea to Egypt, which became an extremely prosperous trading port. By the fourteenth and fifteenth centuries, most of the goods that used to be transported through Baghdad began, instead, to go through Cairo. The Indian Gujerat sea merchants of Bombay were the most influential go-betweens in this trade between the east and west.

From Cairo, Asian goods entered Europe, mainly through the ports of Venice and Genoa, Italy, which competed against each other to monopolize this trade. After the fall of Constantinople in 1453, however, the Ottoman Turks began to threaten to cut off their supplies from Asia. It is argued that a coalition between the Venetians and Genoese might have successfully kept the Turks at bay.[9] Instead, these two cities jealously competed against one another.

The Genoese, after receiving the blessing of the pope in Rome, entered into a secretive and tricky alliance with the Turks, which helped the Ottomans to conquer Venice in 1499. Then, the Turks gained control over Damascus in 1516, and Egypt in the following year.

The occupation of these strategically important overland routes by non-Christian powers did not stop the flow of Asian goods to Europe. Rather, the price of spices became increasingly more expensive for Europeans. Europeans depended on spices to preserve and make their meats and other foods tastier. They grew accustomed to using various spices for medicinal and recreational purposes. Merchants who controlled the ports kept charging higher and higher tolls. Asian goods used to be cheaper when they entered Europe by way of Baghdad and onward through the Syrian coastal towns. However, as trade began to move through Cairo, and the local merchants took a bigger piece of the pie, prices began to spiral. The Turks, for the same political and economic reasons, exacted as much taxes and tribute as the market would bear from this trade. This was one of the reasons that caused the European countries, especially Portugal and Spain, to look for an all-water route to gain direct access to Asian goods.

THE CONQUISTADORS

Portugal and Spain were the first European countries to search for an alternate route of trade to India, China, Japan, and island Southeast Asia. The discovery of the New World by Christopher Columbus in 1492, which paved the way for the discovery of the Philippines by Ferdinand de Magellan in 1521, largely occurred as a result of the high European demand for spices and other goods coming from Asia. Most overland routes were under the control of Muslim powers that charged excessive taxes on goods coming from Asia, which made the price of Asian goods too expensive for Western Europeans. Thus, they felt a need to look for a new all-water route to the East.

In 1488, the Portuguese, led by Bartolomeu Dias, reached the southernmost horn of Africa. This was a great achievement for the Europeans because all of the other routes of trade from the east African coastline to the Indian coastal communities had already been navigated by others. In 1497, the Portuguese, under Vasco da Gama, reached the west coast of India, largely through the navigational skills and guidance of two Gujerat traders whom da Gama brought aboard when sailing along the east African coastline. When da Gama returned home, he received a hero's welcome by the Portuguese people, who quickly assembled a fleet of well-armed ships to exploit this region of the world.

In 1493, Pope Alexander VI issued the Treaty of Tordesillas to keep the relationship between the Portuguese and Spanish harmonious and to prevent them from fighting over new territorial discoveries. Drawing a line from the

North Pole to the South Pole, Pope Alexander VI gave away what was not his to give, all of the land on the east side this line to Portugal, and assigned all of the land on the west side to Spain. At this time, most Europeans accepted and agreed with Nicolaus Copernicus's theory that the earth was round, but they had no idea of the earth's actual size. Most believed that India could be found a short distance over the western horizon of the Atlantic Ocean. Although the Portuguese were the first westerners to control the ancient Asian trade routes, their reign of power ended after a single century. They quickly rose to power by meddling and interfering in the political affairs of other cultures and societies and by taking advantage of rivalries, such as between Hindus and Muslims, which were beginning to occur when the Portuguese arrived. They captured Goa in 1510, Mallacca in 1511, and Hormuz in the Persian Gulf in 1515. The Portuguese conquered Maccau in 1557, and from there they intercepted all sea merchant ships going to the Arab coast.[10] They constructed a series of forts on Ceylon, Ambon, Banda, and Java. But, their empire quickly fell apart. According to some scholars, the Portuguese lost their power for three primary reasons: First, they operated out of the limited territorial expanse of fortresses. Second, they lacked sufficient manpower to control such a big territorial empire. Third, they were mischievous adventurers and profiteers motivated by their own selfish desires for booty and profit.[11]

The Portuguese and, a little later, Spanish committed some grave atrocities against the local people, especially during the early years. Da Gama, on his second trip to India, destroyed a fleet of Muslim ships in the bay of Calicut: "He chopped off the noses, ears, and hands of some eight hundred Moslems and sent them ashore to the Samorin of Calicut with the suggestion to make curry of them."[12] There are many records of abuses committed by the Portuguese. They wielded a policy of terror to intimidate local populations into submission. Their strategy of rule by fear had the reverse effect, however, as more people than before converted to Islam after their arrival.[13]

In contrast to the Portuguese who searched for a new route to the East by following along the African shore always in sight of the land, the Spaniards went directly west out into the dangerous uncharted Atlantic Ocean. On October 12, 1492, Christopher Columbus, an outside Portuguese contractor, discovered America for Spain, although he believed for his entire life that he had discovered outlying islands of India. In the year 1513, seven years after the passing of Columbus, Vasco Nunez de Balboa crossed the Isthmus of Panama, climbed the peak of Darien, and looked down on what appeared to be a new ocean expanse. It was after hearing of his discovery that the Europeans began to realize that they had encountered a new world. September 20, 1519, Spain launched another heavily armed fleet under the command of Ferdinand de Magellan, another Portuguese hireling, to colonize Asia. Magellan sailed across the Atlantic between Africa and Brazil and southward, passing through the straight of Magellan, and on November 28, 1520, came upon the Pacific Ocean. Crossing the Pacific, quelling onboard mutinies, and enduring many hardships and illnesses, such as scurvy and dysentery, Magellan reached the Philippines on March 16, 1521. He initially named these islands Lazarus because, like Lazarus who arose from the dead, his crew survived illness to regain their strength and vitality.[14] Twenty-two years later, Ruy Lopez de Villalobos renamed the islands the Philippines, after King Philip of Spain.

The earliest and most reputable source on Magellan's travels in the Philippines remains the diary of his scribe, Antonio Pigafetta.[15] It is important to remember that when Magellan sailed around the world, the Philippines did not exist on any European map at that time. However, other peoples from around Asia, Arabia, and Persia had already navigated and frequented these islands in ancient times. Magellan first spotted the island of Samar, although he was unable to anchor his ships along its rocky shoreline of steep and overarching cliffs. He continued to sail to nearby Homonhon in the Gulf of Leyte, where he sent his men ashore for rest and recuperation. His sailors were all suffering from scurvy due to lack of vitamin C, but after being taken care of by the local people who fed them meals rich in fruits and vegetables and provided them navigational information, they recovered. After Magellan and his men had regained their strength, they continued to sail southwest, until they reached Masao, Butuan, in Mindanao.[16]

Upon reaching Masao, Magellan was met by a group of emissaries who sailed out to greet him. His slave interpreter, Enrique, beckoned them to come aboard, but they refused. Instead, Enrique and a few of his companions went to meet them on shore. It is interesting to note that Magellan had purchased Enrique some 10 years ago from a slave market in Malacca. Pigafetta reported that Enrique was able to communicate with the local king in the same dialect, much to Magellan's amazement. Enrique was probably a Cebuano because he was the interpreter who provided Pigafetta with the "Malay" words in his journal that actually are Cebuano terms.[17] While it is unknown if Enrique was speaking in Cebuano or another pan-Asian language, it is believed that he may be the first Filipino to have traveled all around the world. Enrique befriended King Kolumbu, who came back with him to meet Magellan, giving him gifts of gold and ginger. In return, Magellan gave the king glass beads and food, while boasting of his arsenal filled with guns and weapons. To impress the king, Magellan even had all his ship's cannons shot off at once, which shocked and frightened the Filipinos, who probably thought that they had better play along with Magellan, rather than get on his bad side. Magellan, having been informed of the local custom, offered to make a blood pact with the king, who complied. This was the first known treaty made between a Filipino king and Western official.

Magellan sent Pigafetta with Enrique and a few others to accompany the king back home. In preparation for their arrival, a fresh pig was roasted and served in their honor. From the local perspective, this was more than merely a meal, though, for to partake in such a feast symbolized a commitment of lifelong friendship. Oral contracts held more weight than written contracts in ancient Asia, and still do in some contexts today. King Kolumbu's brother, King Siaui, informed Pigafetta that there was plenty of gold on the island, "the size of walnuts and eggs," and that even his house was decorated in gold. Pigafetta described the king this way:

> His hair was exceedingly black, and hung to his shoulders. He has a covering of silk on his head, and wore two large golden earrings fastened to his ears. He wore a cotton cloth all embroidered with silk, which covered him from waist to the knees. At his side hung a dagger, the shaft of which was somewhat long and all of gold, and its scabbard of carved wood. He had three spots of gold on every tooth, and his teeth appeared as if bound with gold. He was perfumed with storax and benzoin. He was tawny and painted (tattooed) all over.[18]

Magellan had his men pretend that they were not interested in gold, for he was plotting to return again to steal it. His hosts, generously, shared geographical and cultural knowledge with Magellan and recommended that he sail to Cebu Island to stock up on supplies. King Kolumbu, who offered his free services, went along to show Magellan the way, arriving in Cebu on March 7, 1621.

Cebu was a leading bustling center of trade that produced iron weapons, copper, gold, jewels, textiles, and boats. The local people had long been trading with the Chinese, at least as early as the Tang and Sung dynasties of the tenth and eleventh centuries, and with the Sumatrans and Javanese during the Sri-Vijaya Empire. They were well acquainted with the protocol for receiving foreign dignitaries and merchant guests. When Magellan arrived, the king of Cebu, King Humabon, requested that he provide a gift of tribute, which was a customary gesture of respect for their culture. However, Magellan defiantly replied that "his King was the greatest in all the world and the Armada de Molluca would never pay tribute to a lesser ruler,"[19] which almost incited a fight, but the King of Butuan interceded and offered to speak with the king of Cebu on Magellan's behalf. At the same time, a visiting Siamese guest whispered in the king's ear that Magellan was cut of the same cloth as the Portuguese, who had already raped and pillaged communities further south. Their intercessions caused pause as King Humabon drew the meeting to a close. The next morning, he sent his nephew and future heir bearing tribute and gifts for Magellan as a gesture of peace.

Magellan received the delegation from Cebu with aplomb:

> The Captain General was seated in a red velvet chair, his principal men on leather chairs, and the others on mats upon the floor. The Captain

General asked them, through an interpreter, whether that prince had the authority to make peace. The Captain General said many things concerning peace, and he prayed to God to confirm it in heaven. They said that they never heard such words, but that they took great pleasure in hearing them. The Captain General, seeing that they listened and answered willingly, began to advance an argument to induce them to accept the faith.[20]

His eloquent speech may have impressed some of them, as one prince asked to stay behind to learn more about this faith. Pigafetta noted that Magellan "wept for joy" over this prince and offered to send a priest to instruct and baptize all the Cebuanos. However, Magellan spoke in contradictions: on the one hand, he assured the delegation that only those who freely desired to be converted would be baptized and that no harm would come to the others, while on the other hand, he stipulated that non-Christians would be his enemy.[21]

The king of Cebu invited Magellan to attend a feast in his honor. Arriving, "they found the king seated on a palm mat, with a cotton cloth before his private parts, a scarf embroidered with needle about his head, a necklace of great value around his neck, and two large gold earrings fastened in his ears round with precious gems. He was fat and short, and tattooed with fire of various designs."[22] This description reverberates with descriptions of ancient Hindu kings, as illustriously illustrated in the Mahabharata.[23] From another mat on the ground, he ate turtle eggs, which even today continue to be a delicacy in Cebu, and there were four jars of palm wine, each with a reed straw, covered with sweet-smelling herbs. On approaching the king, Enrique, the interpreter, relayed that Magellan had sent a gift for the king not in direct reciprocation but as a symbol of his true love. Then, they dressed the king in a red velvet robe, donned him with cap, and hung a beaded necklace around his neck. As the ceremonial meal was about to begin, Magellan bowed out with apology and returned to dine alone aboard ship. Pigafetta and several others stayed behind to enjoy the king's hospitality. At nightfall, they were accompanied to a beautiful uplifted bamboo home where three dancing girls awaited. Pigafetta was delighted, saying "they were nearly as white as European girls. They had large holes in their ears with a small piece of wood in the hole. They had long black hair, and wore a short cloth about the head, and were always barefoot. The prince had three quite naked girls dance for us."[24]

The next day, Magellan busied himself with matters of trade and exchange. Also, he supervised the baptismal rites: once the king was baptized, all of his retinue followed. Interestingly, he gave the queen a small statue of Santo Nino, the Christ child, around which legends have grown. For example, if Santo Nino is dislodged from his shrine at Saint Augustine Church located in downtown Cebu City, he will fly back again. He remains the patron saint of Cebu and center of devotional ceremonies and festivities. In 1665, 45 years after Magellan, this same Santo Nino statue was found by a member of Miguel Lopez de Legazpi's expedition. It is one of the oldest known relics of colonial Christianity in the Philippines. A second icon is the cross planted by Magellan that still stands in the courtyard of Saint Augustine Church. After Father Valderrama baptized the king and queen, 2,000 more islanders were baptized. Magellan rounded up and burned holy idols and sacred texts connected with the indigenous belief system. He forced local rulers in nearby villages to recognize the supremacy of King Humabon, and his soldiers systematically burned down the villages of those who resisted, which, needless to say, created enemies.

King Lapu Lapu of Mactan Island refused to be baptized and instead wanted to fight the invaders. Magellan, ignoring the admonitions of even his closest advisers, accepted the challenge and ordered his men to gear up for battle. He was so assured of his own superiority that he ordered Humabon's men to stay out it and observe "how the Spanish lions fought."[25] Pigaffeta recorded this battle:

> Midnight (April 27, 1521), sixty men set out armed with corselets and helmets, together with the Christian king, the prince, and some of the chief men, and twenty or thirty barrangays (large sailing canoes). We reached Mactan, three hours before dawn. The captain did not wish to fight, but a notice to the natives by the Moro (merchant from Siam) to the effect that if they would not obey the king of Spain, recognize the Christian king as their sovereign, and pay us our tribute, he would be their friend; but if they wished otherwise, they would see how our lances wound. They replied that if we had lances, they had lances of bamboo and stakes hardened with fire. When morning came, forty nine of us leaped into the water up to our thighs, and walked through the water for more than two crossbow flights before we could reach the shore. The boats could not approach nearer because of certain rocks in the water. The other eleven men remained behind to guard the boats. When we reached the land, their men had formed in three divisions to number more than one thousand five hundred persons. When they heard us, they charged down upon us with exceedingly loud cries, two divisions on our flanks and the other in our front.[26]

In short, Magellan and his men were surrounded on all sides. His musketeers and crossbowmen shot from a distance but to no avail because the shots merely pierced the wooden shields of the warriors. Meanwhile, the warriors aimed their spears and arrows at the Spaniards bare legs. The battle dragged on, and the Spaniards put up valiant fight, but, in the end, Magellan was mortally wounded. His men went into retreat, and the battle was lost.

Magellan's death may have been a result of his own soldiers not performing their duty. When Magellan landed to confront King Lapu Lapu, the gunners aboard the ships were supposed to cover for him. Possibly, the low tide prevented them from coming closer, but they did not send reinforcements when they saw their captain in trouble. It was the Cebuanos, not the Spaniards, who came for Pigafetta and the other survivors. That is, either the crew members refused to come to Magellan's aid or their own officers ordered them to stay put. His death led to infighting among the officers, and, although Juan Serrano and Duarte Barbosa were elected to lead them, there were dissenters among the ranks. One of them was Enrique, who had been promised his freedom by Magellan. Pigafetta explains that Barbosa told Enrique he was not free and that when they returned to Spain, he would be a slave of Beatriz, Magellan's wife. Enrique reacted by jumping ship.[27]

Pigafetta hypothesized that it was Enrique who conspired to turn Humabon against the Spanish. He probably convinced the king that the Spanish were plotting against him. The day after Magellan's death, King Humabon invited the crew for a banquette. Over 30 men accepted, a quarter of the entire crew, including Barbosa and Serrano. Pigafetta, wounded in battle, stayed behind. Recovering onboard, he awoke in horror to the cries and moans of his crewmen being slaughtered on shore. Twenty-seven died, while the priest and Serrano were captured. A few swam back to the ship, and they prepared to sail. The Cebuanos brought Serrano out and offered to exchange him for ransom. The ransom consisted of an iron gun, but as soon as this was given, they asked for more. This continued until the men onboard gave up, despite Serrano's pleas, and, concludes Pigafetta, he was probably killed like the rest.

The remaining crew members sailed around the southern Philippines looking for directions to the Moluccas, the Spice Islands (Indonesia). Once there, they repaired their ships and sailed homeward to Seville, Spain, arriving on May 6, 1521.

Over the next 50 years, Spain sent out four expeditions to the Philippines, which culminated in the expedition of Miguel Lopez de Legazpi, who returned to take possession of Cebu in 1565. Resil Mojares[28] found that Cebu Island had by then become so prosperous that the Spaniards decided to develop it into an administrative, military, and religious center for the Philippines. However, they quickly abandoned their plans and transferred their base of operations to Panay in 1569 and then Manila. They retracted their plans due to the rapid economic decline on the island that resulted in the lack of any real economic opportunities for Cebuanos under Spanish rule. In addition, the Spaniards were ill prepared and lacked the necessary resources to defend themselves against increasing attacks by sea marauders, including, but not exclusively, the Portuguese who stormed through early on. Even after moving their base to Manila, the Spaniards were never as interested as were the pre-Hispanic Chinese traders in purchasing Cebu's total output of raw cotton but purchased only high-priced specialty products, such as *lampotes*, and only enough to fill a single galleon that made an annual voyage between Cebu and Mexico.[29] This change led Cebu's southern farmers to shift to cultivating Indian corn, which continues to be the main staple crop of these Cebuanos even to present because it could be cultivated in soil already infertile due to its having been planted in cotton. Cebu's economy deteriorated from the development of Manila-centered galleon trade with China and Mexico, which effectively blocked Cebu's commerce for almost 200 years. Its economy continued to change in relation to Spain and the incipient Western world market system.

IMPACT OF COLONIAL CHRISTIANITY

The Spanish conquistadors, administrators, and missionaries came to the Philippine islands with preconceptions of paganism, conquest, and mission based on unrealistic Augustinian and Greco-Roman definitions of Barbarians. While the Filipinos had long traded with peaceful merchants and aggressive marauders offering protection in return for tribute, they were never really prepared for the abrupt and arbitrary appearance of the conquistadors. Although Muslims had penetrated the islands to such a degree that the Tagalogs in the far north had been won for that faith, and as much as Islam like Christianity was an intolerant religion, it did not predispose the Filipinos for the arrival of Christianity. The Muslims were not able to exercise the same type of center-to-periphery control that Spain could at least attempt. That is, the Roman Catholic Church was hierarchically organized and emanated out from Rome, under the rule of the Pope. By contrast, the Muslim world system of the day was much more loose and multicentered. The Europeans only imagined that the Ottomans exercised any influence in Asia. The spread of Islam depended on the formation of many local states, not a single "world empire" that Spain was becoming.

The Spaniards negotiated their terms of settlement predominantly through the agency of male leaders, while female leaders, who held positions of high esteem and authority in the bilateral contexts of the precolonial Philippines, were displaced. The lord-to-vassal relationship in Southeast Asia differed substantially from that of Spain. Differences in gender roles were simply differences in work patterns that complemented each other to form an undifferentiated whole. Some scholars stress that the early Filipino ideology of gender differences was complementary.[30] The opposite sexes complimented each other rather than competed against each other. In Southeast Asia, a follower system (still) is the realization that a relation of authority of high over low exists and, likewise, the understanding that teachers and students, masters and disciples, need each other in striving for ascendancy.[31] This relation is based on cooperation, not competition. On the other hand, the relation between equal groups such as in the United States or contemporary capitalist-led global politics is best described as opposition. Spanish colonial policy attempted to solidify local leadership and, in effect, transform local leaders into permanent lower-level authority figures solidified in power by the Crown, so long as the indigenous elite cooperated. Researchers say that "the extension of Spanish colonial rule into local communities generated a new division between natives who paid tribute and natives who collected it."[32] The indigenous elite now sanctioned by outside military force could opportunistically shift between colonial overlords and their subjects. They could take surplus from a community and keep part of it for themselves in the form of goods or indentured servitude. Although the local leaders were accorded land and freed from tribute and corvée labor by the Spaniards, their prior wealth and power derived less from the land than from tribute and services rendered by their followers. The Spanish government undermined the indigenous economic system by exacting head taxes on all commoners. They accomplished this through warfare and Catholic indoctrination and conversion. Subjects fled from both tax collectors and former rulers or, when prevented from doing so, rebelled.

Spanish colonizers systematically brought the Filipinos, whom they called "Indios," into *encomiendas*. *Encomiendas* were settlements of local people created by the Spaniards for purposes of assessment and tax collection. The holistic cultures of the early Filipinos were fragmented by this forced relocation process. The precolonial communities reflected the particular lifestyles of their residents as petty traders, horticulturalists, and hunters and gatherers. As the conquerors reduced them into fixed settlements, they had to adopt European ways of seeing and dividing the world. Filipinos had to grapple with the problem of losing their cultural identity and communal orientation due to the foreign nature of the Spanish language and ways. They were required to perform corvée labor and pay tribute. It is believed that "dependency and indebtedness characterized this multifaceted relationship" between the Spaniards and Filipinos. "At best it gave way to a paternalistic relationship, at worst it created an exploitative set up."[33] As we shall see in chapter 4, this relationship would intensify when the American colonizers brought their capitalist mode of production at the turn of the twentieth century and transformed the instrumental overlord-to-peasant relationship into an instrumental impersonal relationship based on paid labor.

The Spanish, who transmitted the Christian faith, held in common the other-worldly and future-oriented conceptions of the Bible, while the Filipinos interpreted the scriptures more in a present-oriented and experiential way. Religion was real only as it could be experienced and seen in the manifestations of God's love in the world. For example, his love was expressed in the tangible form of rain that nourished a community garden. The Spanish colonization process attempted to reconstruct the core of Filipino ideology and social life. Spain's presence in the Philippines could only be legitimated as a function of the Christianizing mission, and the Filipinos were forced to reorient themselves in relation to a divine authority whose directives came from Spain. Instead of situating themselves in relation to Southeast Asia and the natural world around them, Filipinos "were constrained to negotiate with and around the totalitarian economy of divine mercy."[34] The prior system of relating to others in terms of mutual indebtedness and exchange was replaced by one of divine patronage tied to the bureaucracy of colonial Spain. Local autonomy was lost.

Filipinos and friars localized Christianity for economic and political reasons. The priest used his role as father confessor to force his parishioners into debt and further dependence upon him.[35] By such means, the Filipinos were led to obey their Spanish overlords. While religious clergy no doubt served to domesticate potentially unruly and landless laborers for Filipino and Spanish officials, a rather different interpretation of confession is given by De la Costa, who suggests that this sacrament could also be used to oversee Spanish abuse of power. In fact, the early Spanish abuse of Filipinos was so offensive to some Catholic friars that the first bishop of the Philippines, Bishop Salazar, called for a meeting of a synod in Manila in 1581. Describing the times, the Spanish bishop thundered that "it was absurd that a man of low degree, merely because he immigrates to the colonies, should acquire the prerogatives of a knight and lord of vassals, doing violence and a thousand injustices to the miserable native who is unable to stand his ground against the arrogance of the Spaniard and the tyranny of his own chiefdoms."[36] Under the new synod directives, absentee *encomenderos,* in particular, were found guilty. Similarly, Spanish troops and other laymen who committed crimes against the Filipinos were ordered to compensate their victims, though there was scant way to enforce this directive. The proceedings from the synod were drawn up in a handbook for priests to use in the confessional to oversee *encomenderos* and conquistadors. The directives, however, were not well received, and the offenders simply stopped going to confession.

Others counter that while some friars accused the *encomenderos* of exorbitant exactions and other abuses, some governors complained that the friars had "exploited and reduced the natives to virtual slavery."[37] But if Filipinos wished to report the misdeeds of their friars and overlords to the civil authorities, they had to do so through the agency of another friar. The system was corruptible. Only rarely did clerics take a real stand to protect their parishioners' rights. It was not even until the latter part of the nineteenth century that select members of the Chinese mestizo and Filipino *illustrado* class were for the first time admitted into the priesthood, so, before then, the indigenous people could not represent themselves in Spanish courts because they could not enter the priesthood. This is in contrast to the Muslim and Buddhist development of an indigenous religious elite. The first council of Mexico (1555) forbade Indios, mestizos, and mulattoes to enter the priesthood because they "resembled the descendents of the Moors and persons who had been sentenced by the Inquisition as lacking in good repute which those who bear the sacerdotal character ought to have," an indictment repeated in milder form at the second council of Mexico in 1585.[38] While Catholic clerics willingly allowed themselves to be used by rich patrons, over time some spoke out against social injustices, such as those who sermonized against the authorities of the church and Crown in 1768, when the pope ordered the Jesuits to return to Spain. Although some peasants got attached to their priests through rituals such as processions and novenas to petition for a good harvest or cures, the localization of Christianity still partly occurred in relation to precolonial Southeast Asian history in a process multisided and complex.

On the one hand, many early missionaries taught a mystified and other-worldly version of Christianity to indoctrinate and subdue the masses for their conquerors. They misled Filipinos to redress felt wrongs through appeal to a higher other-worldly God, rather than to social and economic conditions stemming from the inequitable relationship of the imperialists to the colonized. Both friars and collaborating local elites were accomplices in this coercive conversion that rested more on tenets of Hispanicization than Christianization. However, it must be remembered that Filipinos, simultaneously, interpreted Christianity in terms of traditional Southeast Asian cultural beliefs and practices. Many articulated the language of Christianity as a means for expressing their own values, ideals, and hopes for liberation from their colonial oppressors. While colonial Christianity profoundly influenced and changed the historical development of the Philippines, Filipino communities had encountered and modified many different religious and cultural influences before in their long history. It seems natural that many would make their own interpretations of the scriptures to contest and later transform Spanish rule.

Undoubtedly, the Spanish colonization processes had a disintegrating effect on the indigenous political economy. The Spanish disrupted traditional values, communal practices, and social relations by instituting a new class structure that served the colonial interests and that undermined the preexisting maritime trade economy. They brought with them a feudalistic production mode that restructured trade and labor. Land that was held in common was increasingly reduced to private property. This instigated a process of eroding the traditional subsistence base and created a class of dispossessed peasants. By the nineteenth century, as we shall see in the next chapter, however, cash cropping for sugar, tobacco, rubber, and other crops by expropriating Filipino labor and resources began to transform the productive base in such a way as to allow the emergence of a small class of landed and entrepreneurial Filipino and Chinese families, from whom emerged powerful religious and political leaders. This increasingly educated and internationalized class of Filipino elites began to play a formative role in helping to shape popular ideas and opinions opposing the prevailing order. Under these divergent conditions of production, the Philippine Independence Movement from colonial rule emerged.

NOTES

1. Nicolas Zafra, *The Colonization of the Philippines and the Beginnings of the Spanish City in Manila* (Manila: National Historical Institute, 1993), p. 4.

2. William Henry Scott, *Slavery in the Spanish Philippines* (Manila: De La Salle University Press, 1991), p. 12.

3. William Henry Scott, *Barangay* (Quezon City: Ateneo de Manila Press, 1999), p. 127–128.

4. Stephen Lansing, *The Balinese* (San Diego: Harcourt Brace, 1997).

5. William Henry Scott, *Barangay*, p. 231.

6. Vincente Rafael, *Contracting Colonialism Translation and Christian Conversion in Tagalog Society under Early Spanish Rule* (Ithaca: Cornell University Press, 1988), p. 106.

7. John Phelan, *The Hispanization of the Philippines* (Madison: University of Wisconsin Press, 1959).

8. The Chinese system of acupuncture and herbal healing was at its pinnacle during the Middle Ages. The Chinese invented firecrackers, which westerners later used as gun powder. Koreans invented the first printing blocks to mass-produce one of the earliest compilations of Mahayana Buddhism that was recorded by Korean monks who studied under Buddhist teachers in ancient Ceylon, now called Sri Lanka.

9. George Massleman, *The Cradle of Colonialism* (New Haven: Yale University Press, 1963), chap. 11.

10. George Massleman, *The Cradle of Colonialism*, p. 221.

11. George Massleman, *The Cradle of Colonialism*, p. 223.

12. George Massleman, *The Cradle of Colonialism*, p. 218.

13. George Massleman, *The Cradle of Colonialism*, p. 209.

14. Laurence Bergreen, *Over the Edge of the World* (New York: Harper Perennial, 2003), p. 239.

15. Antonio Pigaffeta's journals are primary documents that have been widely translated and used by historians and biographers of Ferdinand Magellan to better understand his trip around the world. A recent rendition, with reference to the Philippines and that is rich in detail and partly informs this section, can be found in Laurence Bergreen's "A Vanished Empire" and "The Final Battle" in *Over the Edge of the World*, chaps. 9 and 10.

16. Sonia Zaide, ed., *Butuan, The First Kingdom* (Butuan City: Artop Printing House, 1990). In this archeological publication, Sonia Zaide documents that Magellan first landed on what has proved to be the island of Butuan, not Limasawa. Butuan is located on the nine and two-thirds degrees north latitude,

which is the position located by Pigafetta. Pigafetta's account is considered the most reliable account of Magellan's voyage. Other primary accounts by survivors of Magellan's trip are not in agreement about the location where he first landed in the Philippines, after leaving the atoll of Homonhon.

17. Dr. Frederico Magdalena (personal communication 2007) with the Center for Philippine Studies at the University of Hawaii, Manoa, theorizes that Enrique must have been a Cebuano-speaking person since he was the one who supplied the "Malay" words, which Pigafetta enthusiastically encoded in his annals. To see some of these words, interested readers are referred to http://www.language-links.org/fil.cwrd.html.

18. Sonia Zaide, ed. *Butuan, The First Kingdom*, p. 7.

19. Laurence Bergreen, *Over the Edge of the World*, pp. 257–258.

20. Laurence Bergreen, *Over the Edge of the World*, pp. 259–260.

21. Laurence Bergreen, *Over the Edge of the World*, pp. 260, 269.

22. Laurence Bergreen, *Over the Edge of the World*, pp. 261–264.

23. The Mahabharata is an ancient mythological story of the birth of India.

24. Laurence Bergreen, *Over the Edge of the World*, p. 263.

25. Laurence Bergreen, *Over the Edge of the World*, p. 276.

26. Nicolas Zafra, *The Colonization of the Philippines and the Beginnings of the Spanish City in Manila*, p. 21.

27. Laurence Bergreen, *Over the Edge of the World*, p. 293.

28. Resil Mojares, "The Formation of a City: Trade and Politics in Nineteenth-Century Cebu," in *The Philippine Quarterly of Culture and Society*, Vol. 19, No. 1 (1991), p. 288.

29. Joseph Baumgartner, "Cotton—A Pre-Spanish Cebuano Industry: Facts and Problems," in *The Philippine Quarterly of Culture and Society*, Vol. 3 (1975), p. 40.

30. Sherry Errington, "Recasting Gender and Power: A Theoretical and Regional Overview," in *Power and Difference: Gender in Island Southeast Asia*, ed. Sherry Errington (Stanford: Stanford University Press, 1990).

31. Anthony Reid, *Slavery, Bondage and Dependency in Southeast Asia* (New York: St. Martin's Press, 1983), p. 7.

32. Vincente Rafael, *Contracting Colonialism*, pp. 13–17.

33. Wilfredo Fabros, *The Church and Its Social Involvement in the Philippines, 1930–1972* (Quezon City: Ateneo de Manila Press, 1988), p. 5.

34. Vincente Rafael, *Contracting Colonialism*, p. 109.

35. Vincente Rafael, *Contracting Colonialism*, p. 99.

36. H. de la Costa, *The Jesuits in the Philippines, 1581–1768* (Cambridge: Harvard University Press, 1961), p. 33.

37. Renato Constantino, *The Philippines: A Past Revisited* (Quezon City: Tala Press, 1975), pp. 22, 77–78.

38. H. de la Costa, *The Jesuits in the Philippines, 1581–1768*, pp. 233–235.

3

The Philippine Revolution (1896–1902)

The Spaniards had three primary objectives in colonizing the Philippines. One was to gain a share of the profitable spice trade dominated by the Portuguese in south and Southeast Asia. The second was to establish a stopover in the galleon trade between Mexico and China, with the intention of setting up a home base for the evangelization of China and Japan. The third was to Christianize the people of the Philippines. After establishing the capital in Manila, Spanish officials had little interest in developing the countryside and largely confined their activities to the galleon trade coming out of the capital city, while the friars established themselves on agricultural lands. Aside from the big landed estates, most of the communities in the countryside were based on a subsistence economy. These communities consisted of self-provisioning households that also met the material needs of the small nonproducing colonial population. The Spaniards divided the land into *encomiendas,* or settlement communities, by bringing together several villages around a church center, initially under the control of a conquistador and, soon after, the religious orders. In exchange for their participation in governance, the friars and other administrators who helped to run the colony, were granted the right to levy tribute and require labor. Much of life in the countryside carried on as usual in accordance to local customs and traditions for the first 200 years of Spanish rule. The Philippines, except Manila, was largely closed from the outside world.

However, economic and political changes in Europe beginning in the eighteenth century affected the Philippines. The Industrial Revolution begun in England extended and transformed Europe into highly productive and resource-consuming nations competing for new sources of raw materials and markets for their surplus products. This cued Spain to restructure the Philippine economy by promoting logging, mining, and mono-cropping for export, which hastened the integration of the local economy into the European market system. This restructuring process, combined with increasing land grabbing by the friars and colonial elites, fueled the grounds for revolution, as did the inflow of liberal ideas and enlightened attitudes, especially after the Spanish Revolution of 1869. The increased speed and easement of transportation after the completion of the Suez Canal in 1868 opened new opportunities for an ambitious and newly emerging landed class of Filipinos to further their education at home and abroad. Internationalized intellectuals and progressive Filipino priests called for governmental reform and the secularization of the church. The harsh reprisals made by the Spanish government against these reformists, especially the martyrdom of Fathers Gomez, Burgos, and Zamora in 1872 and of the nationalist writer, Jose Rizal in 1896, inspired Philippine nationalism and the revolts of the nineteenth century.

BACKGROUND

One of the most striking features of the Spanish colonial system was the union of church and state, the Spanish Crown having been vested by the Holy See with the charge of operating the missions in the new colonies. The state provided the military protection and political organization, and the church took care of the spiritual consolidation of the people to keep them under control. Once Spain established her base of operations in Manila in 1571, she developed it into a major naval station in the Pacific. Her goal was to gain a foothold in the spice trade that was dominated by the Portuguese, and later, the Dutch, by making Manila the transshipment port in the galleon trade between Mexico and China. For the first 200 years, Spain had little interest in developing agriculture or other resources in the archipelago. She monopolized trade by dictating that all galleons coming out of the country had to pass first through Manila. This trade was Spain's major source of income and economic activity. So, the communities in the countryside were delegated to the religious orders to organize and implement a new governing apparatus.

The galleon trade operated on three levels. The Chinese traded silks, teas, and spices for Philippine rice, abaca, and tobacco, and Mexican silver. Each year, one galleon sailed to Acapulco, Mexico, carrying in its hold Chinese silks, teas, and spices, and returned with 100 to 300 percent profits in Mexican silver. The Crown restricted the galleon to one trip a year in an effort to prevent silver from draining out of her empire. The profits from this trade and the regular annuity coming from Mexico paid for all government expenses. The Manila–Acapulco trade was so profitable that it motivated the conquistadors and colonial officials to concentrate exclusively on acquiring and filling a space in the hold of the ship, since they could expect to live comfortably off the profits for the rest of the year.

The Spanish first implemented a system of indirect rule by appointing local kings and princes as provincial governors or village heads. This method of using local leaders under colonial rule effected a significant change in their status, as their positions, now reinforced by the state, were more firmly inherited and devoid of power. After subordinating their authority to that of the friars to whom they turned to for protection against the arbitrary demands and sporadic acts of cruelty committed by the Spanish soldiers and governing officials, indigenous political and economic rulers were transformed into little more than tribute collectors. They no longer held sway over followers who rebelled, fled, or rejected the colonial order from within.

Another group of people whose power was diminished by Christianity included the shamans and priestesses of the ancient Philippine societies. It is suggested that the early friars slandered and maligned priestesses in an effort to negate the power of these women and institute a religious conversion of the island population. The friars transposed the shamans into witches so as to discredit them locally. This is further substantiated on the basis that the myth of the human viscera sucker is found mainly in the Christian lowlands, especially the Visayas and Bicol regions, not the non-Hispanicized uplands of northern Luzon and Mindanao.[1] One scholar, Cristina Blanc-Szanton, discusses the changing status of women in relation to the Spanish colonization process.[2] William Henry Scott's work is replete with examples of precolonial women who enjoyed a politically and economically more balanced relationship with their men than did their European counterparts.[3] H. de la Costa wrote between the lines that women played more vital social roles as healers, warrior priestesses, and merchants before the colonial period. Female merchants swam out to meet the Spanish ships when they first arrived. Female shamans performed the role of midwives and healers. They rallied forth and accompanied their men into rebellion against Spanish overlords.[4] Spanish Catholics with their dark and repressed attitudes toward sexuality were shocked by the Filipinos' easy-going manners when it came to sexual behavior.[5] This is not to say that precolonial Filipinos did not have high societal mores and rules governing marriage practices, but rather, they were more comfortable with expressing and being fully themselves than were the European colonizers.

Spanish colonization changed everything about early Filipino society. The colonizers so vilified female medicine women and priestesses that they called them witches or *aswangs*. The Filipino term *aswang* mainly refers to five types of supernatural creatures: the corpse eater who steals and devours corpses; the bloodsucker who sucks out its victim's blood; the flying half-ling who divides its body and leaves its lower sexual parts behind to fly in search of victims to suck out their viscera; the shape shifter, which changes its appearance from human to animal, like a pig or dog, to catch its prey; and the vindictive hex caster who may be a real human being possessing magical powers to inflict harm on others who have offended him or her. Flying half-creatures or *aswangs* can take their position, in the dead of night, atop a roof and extend their tongue in a threadlike form to suck out the blood and entrails of a sick person or newborn infant. They can do harm to the fetuses of a pregnant women. Leading shaman priestesses, with their large followings, were perceived by the Spanish to be powerful competitors. So, as a way to diminish their power and authority, the friars went after them by demonizing and falsely labeling these women as *aswangs* (witches), much as women healers and shamans were degraded in Europe.

After a while, the Spanish friars disposed all of the traditional leaders by banishing or destroying those who refused to submit to Christianity. They developed large tracts of land that were first granted to the conquistadors and early settlers that were soon turned over to the missionary orders. The Jesuits, Augustinians, Dominicans, and Recollects participated in this aspect of the colonization process. The Augustinians arrived with Miguel Lopez de Legazpi in 1565, which marked the beginning of the long collaboration between the Crown and the Catholic Church in the colonization of the islands. Then, the Franciscans entered in 1577, the Jesuits in 1581, the Dominicans in 1605, and the Recollects in 1606. Only the Franciscans did not actively participate in this land-grabbing enterprise because of their vow of poverty. At first, the friars developed large tracts of agricultural land that supplied rice for local consumption and urban centers, especially Manila. Farming was done by sharecroppers, who the friars were able to recruit by releasing them from tribute-labor demands by the state. The friar estates spread out to encompass more common lands and family plots, which sometimes caused peasant uprisings,[6] such as erupted between 1745 and 1746 in Bulacan, Batangas, Laguna, and Cavite.[7] By the eighteenth century, most of the workers on the friar estates had become tenant farmers who handed over a portion of the harvest as a form of rent. By the latter part of the next century, the religious orders owned some 171,000 hectares of prime agricultural land.[8]

Also, by the eighteenth century, new political and economic developments in Europe, especially the Industrial Revolution in England, caused Spain to reorient her colonial policy in the Philippines. The galleon trade was isolating Manila from world trade that could be useful to its economic development. Even the trip from Manila to Acapulco and back had become very dangerous. For example, the British captured four galleons: the *Santa Ana* in 1587, the *Encarnacio* in 1709, the *Covadonga* in 1743, and the *Santisima Trinidad* in 1762. Spain assessed a need for a commercial system that would develop the country's resources for world trade, but her plans were cut short in 1762 when the British invaded and occupied Manila, which was not restored to Spain until after the signing of the 1763 Paris Peace Treaty. After the British departed, the Spanish colonial government began to promote national development and opened many of the old city ports around the country to international trade. At the same time, the Spaniards became more repressive in dealing with those who called for social, political, and economic reforms. They especially retaliated against the Chinese community in Manila because they welcomed and supported the British troops. Many Chinese were exiled or deported when the Spanish colonial government returned. Also, the Chinese were prohibited from moving around the country, and Chinese immigration to the Philippines was closed until 1840.

Meanwhile, a new class of leading families or *principalia* emerged who helped to govern the towns under the watch of the local friar. These elites, at the beginning, were Spanish mestizos who could trace their descent to a Spaniard who intermarried with a family member. There were five main social strata: the Spanish from Spain who ran the government and religious hub at the center of the colonial administration, the Spanish born in the Philippines and the Spanish mestizos, the Chinese mestizos, the Filipinos divided into the *principalia* and the laboring class, and the Chinese. The *principalia* were educated and well assimilated into the Spanish culture and society. When the peasants suffered severe hardships or in times of natural disasters, they would ask these families, who were often related in some way, for assistance in the form of a loan. The peasants would even sell their land, under an agreement that they could repurchase it within a designated number of years. They could continue to live in their own homes and farm but, now, had a mortgage. It was difficult for them to ever pay off this kind of mortgage because, whenever the next crisis occurred, they could simply refinance but incurred an even bigger debt. Over time, many lost their land completely to the *principalia* class and stayed on to work for them as sharecroppers. This process of disenfranchising people from their land further ripened the ground of rebellion and discontent.

A second class of leading elites who came into being during the late colonial period was the Chinese mestizos. The origins and rise of these leading families can be explained as follows: The early Spanish banned their own merchants from doing business in foreign ports, so the Chinese traders, especially from Fukien and Kwantung, desiring Mexican silver, established themselves instead in the Philippines, especially around Manila and places like Cebu in the central Philippines. Although there were many Chinese in the country before the Spanish arrived, the new wave of immigrants multiplied, especially in the Manila region, and came to outnumber the local Spanish population. The Spaniards felt threatened and reacted defensively by trying to malign their character and spreading false rumors about the poor quality of their products. Many Chinese simply moved out to the countryside, such as Pampanga in central Luzon, where they rented land from the *principalia* and set up sugar mills and other concessions that produced products in high demand for sale in Manila. By the late eighteenth century, these Chinese had successfully blended in and intermarried with the *principalia* and expanded their businesses into export agriculture.[9]

Significantly, the Spanish were never able to fully colonize the Muslim-controlled south, particularly Mindanao and Sulu.[10] Also, the mountain communities around the country offered safe haven and a base for the resistance against colonialism. While the Spanish military invaded parts of Mindanao in 1578–1595, 1630–1650, 1718–1762, and the second half of the nineteenth century, they never stayed long or won over the populous to their faith. After the Spanish began operations in the southern islands, there was a countermovement that triggered a new wave of local conversions to Islam. Each time the Spaniards succeeded in building a fort, such as in Zamboanga, as they did several times, the Jesuits began to Christianize the people. But as soon as the troops left, such as when they were called back to defend the capital city of Manila when it was under attack by the British in 1762, the local people quickly reverted to their former faith and practices. It is argued that the colonial efforts in the southern Philippines have to be analyzed in relation to Spain's military engagements in the region, especially with the Dutch.[11] As Spain colonized the Visayas and Luzon, the Muslim communities in the south intensified and accelerated their efforts to develop stronger political and economic ties with other sultanates in Southeast Asia. This is illustrated by the Maguindanao sultanate of Cotabato that became a formidable sovereign power to contend with during the reign of Sultan Kudarat (1619–1671). He negotiated a trade alliance with the Dutch Trading Company based in Indonesia and supplied them with rice and slaves. Sultan Kudarat and his friend and ally the Sultan of Sulu engaged in slave-raiding expeditions up and down the coasts of the Visayan Islands. He even negotiated a peaceful trading settlement with Spain, which was remarkable since Cotabato was considered to be part of the Spanish Empire. However, by the late eighteenth century, the Spanish navy blocked the river way to the port of Cotabato and successfully cut the Maguindanao off from international trade. This strategic maneuver of war had little effect on the Muslim trade routes, though, because the center swiftly moved to the Sulu sultanate off the coast of southern Mindanao and to other Muslim communities further upriver, which began to multiply and grow into stronger adversaries. Spain was never able to effectively colonize and gain a foothold over Mindanao.

THE REVOLUTION AGAINST SPAIN (1896–1898)

Spain's intentions from the beginning were to replace the friars with secular parish priests whenever any mission assumed the character of a parish. But the friars, not wanting to loose their power and possessions, fought secularization, and it was never carried out entirely. The friars became the storm center of the gradually increasing Filipino demand for change; the revolution of 1896 was principally directed against them. During the first half of the nineteenth century, there were only 2,000 to 5,000 Spaniards in the country. Spanish was spoken only by a few of the people, principally in Manila and a few other important centers, but the friars made little effort to educate the populous. There were many different ethnic and cultural groups that spoke different languages. Partly because of these conditions, the Filipinos had little representation in the Spanish courts and had to have a friar to represent them. But, by the nineteenth century, everything changed as Christianity united Filipinos and the Catholic schools and seminaries had produced a significant number of educated Filipino lay and religious leaders, especially males, who as *principalia* and diocesan priests shared certain advantages with the friars in the rural communities. Children of Filipino-Spanish marriages gradually accumulated large tracts of land and began to develop sugar plantations and so forth. Mestizos of the early conquistadors inherited large estates and sent their children to schools in Spain and Europe, and developed a social and cultural orientation patterned after that of Spain.

However, the Filipinos, no matter how brilliant or well educated, remained outside of the upper echelons of the ruling circles in colonial society. They could never hope to achieve a higher political position that would give them the power to create and envision new structural changes that would benefit Filipinos. Their social, cultural, economic, and political engagements were always guided by the friars. In addition, the conditions of the peasants had worsened with the demise of the galleon trade, which created a need for new sources of revenue, as the landlords and tax collectors went out to exact more taxes, tribute, and labor from the peasantries.

At the same time, the evolving idea of Filipino nationalism began to manifest itself through the Propaganda Movement. *La Solidaridad* was founded by Graciano Lopez Jaena in 1888, and throughout its course urged reforms both in religion and government. One of its foremost contributors was Jose Rizal y Mercado. The Propaganda Movement gained ascendance in the 1880s, when the Filipino students in Spain participated in conferences and literary competitions and projected Philippine realities. Their aim was to expose the deplorable conditions of Philippine society and demonstrate that Filipinos were as intellectually able as anyone else in art, literature, and the humanities. The European colonizers thought that they themselves were a superior race, but this was a fallacy, and the Filipino Christians believed that all men and women were created equal under God and acted accordingly. Filipino artists, the most famous being Juan Luna y Novicio and Felix Resurrection Hidalgo, won various artistic and literary competitions. Jose Rizal published *Noli Me Tangere*[12] and *El Filibusterismo*, and several other award winning essays and poems.

The Filipinos had plenty of reason to complain, especially after 1872. In that year, some 200 soldiers at the Cavite arsenal revolted and called for independence. Plans for a similar demonstration in Manila failed. The revolt was subdued, and mass arrests followed. About sixty conspirators were executed, and others received prison sentences or exile papers. Suspecting that the mutiny was a colony-wide conspiracy to overthrow Spanish colonialism, government officials implicated Fathers Gomez, Burgos, and Zamora, bribing a Bicol ex-soldier, Francisco Zaldua, to testify against them. Convicted, the three priests were garroted to death on the Luneta on February 1, 1872. Their memory became the rallying cry of the Filipino student movement in Spain, which carried on the propaganda campaign and agitated for reform and the revolution of the 1890s. Rizal dedicated his second novel, *El Filibusterismo* (Filibusterism), to them. He wrote:

> The church by refusing to unfrock you, has put in doubt the crime charges against you; the Government by enshrouding your trial in mystery and pardoning your co-accused has implied that some mistake was committed when your fate was decided; and the whole of the Philippines in paying homage to your memory and calling you martyrs totally rejects your guilt. As long therefore as it is not clearly shown that you took part in the uprising at Cavite, and I have the right, whether or not your patriots and whether or not you were seeking justice and liberty, to dedicate my work to you as victims of the evil I am trying to fight. And while we wait for Spain to clear your name someday, refusing to be party to your death, let these pages serve as a belated wreath of withered leaves on your forgotten graves. Whoever attacks your memory without sufficient proof has your blood on their hands.[13]

After the Cavite revolt, the authorities began to arrest, imprison, exile, or execute anyone suspected of organizing antigovernment activities or who even spoke out against the government. Many Filipino activists went into voluntary exile abroad. Since they were powerless to improve conditions at home and risked arrest if they voiced their complaints, they publicized their grievances and aspirations through literary means. The Propaganda Movement, led by Rizal, Marcelo del Pilar, Lopez Jaena, and Apolinario Mabini, continued to grow into a strong protest movement against the domination of the friars and economic and administrative caciques. The movement was supported by a few sympathetic governors, but others, especially the friars, continued to diametrically oppose it. After Rizal returned home from Spain in 1892, he founded an organization called Liga Filipina. He was soon labeled a subversive by the Spanish regime and banished to Dapitan, Zamboanga.

Around the same time that Rizal founded Liga Filipina, another organization, "The Most Respectful Association of the Sons of the People," or Katipunan, was established by Andre Bonifacio on July 7, 1892. In his book *Bonifacio's Unfinished Revolution*, Alejo Villanueva Jr. suggests that the name *Katipunan* represented an invitation to the people to unite for a common purpose. It spoke to the sons and daughters of the country who in their hearts and souls felt filial affection for the motherland and were patriots. Initially, it was a secret society, but soon the triangle system of recruitment wherein one member of each cell would know only one member in the next cell, was replaced by enlistment and organization on the basis of the Liga Filipina. The Katipunan began in the Tagalog region and was composed of the dispossessed lower urban class who could never hope to gain a higher education, advance economically, or enter the ruling classes, other than through revolution. It is estimated to have reached, at some point, between 100,000 to 400,000 members. The society promoted the idea that the Philippines had a long and glorious history before the onslaught of the colonization process. It had an organized state at the time when the Spanish first arrived, conducted international trade, had its own religion and alphabet, and had independence and liberty. They charged that the friars had not really civilized the Filipinos but had taught them a mystified and formulaic version of Christianity. They strove to create a nationalist ideology and independent state by means of revolution.

The Katipunan grew steadily, and one of the objectives of this organization was to fight for independence from Spain. Andre Bonifacio, who admired Jose Rizal, secretly sent an emissary to Dapitan to ask for his support, but Rizal refused. He thought that the Filipino people were not yet prepared intellectually, politically, economically, and militarily for revolution. Also, he did not want to be rescued, because he wanted to keep his word, as he promised the Spanish that he would not leave. Meanwhile, the Katipunan members were busy preparing for revolution. The Spanish authorities learned of the existence of the Katipunan through a friar of Tondo, and Bonifacio and the others fled into hiding in Balintawak, a hilly town northeast of Manila. There they decided to fight for freedom, and symbolically tore their residence certificates, shouting "Mabuhay ang Filipinas! Mabuhay ang mga Filipino!" (Long live the Philippines! Long live the Filipinos!), which became the battle cry for freedom that still burns in the hearts of Filipino patriots.

On August 26, 1896, the center of the revolution broke out in Cavite province, where General Emilio Aguinaldo arose as the new leader who replaced Bonifacio.[14] Spain sent over reinforcements until there was an army of 28,000 besides a few loyal Filipino regimens. The Filipinos greatly outnumbered the Spaniards by as much as 2,000 to 1, but they had only bolos (blades) and a few rifles. The Spanish had far superior weapon power but didn't know how to fight against an enemy who blended in with the local population and who attacked and fought when least expected, especially at night. The fierce fighting went on for 52 days, until everything hit a quagmire. The Spaniards had indiscriminately rounded up and imprisoned hundreds of men; many were tortured. Many more were sent to the Spanish penal colony in Africa. The Spanish authorities committed many atrocities and massacres in their desperation to subdue the rebellion; they terrorized the local population in an attempt to instill fear.[15] In greater Manila, the cells of Fort Santiago and the Bilibid Prison were overcrowded. For example, 169 prisoners were stuffed together beneath the Bastion of San Diego, which had only one small air hole for ventilation. On one rainy night, a soldier closed the air hole to keep out the rain, and, the next day, 54 prisoners were found suffocated to death. The Spanish authorities ironically arrested Jose Rizal and falsely indicted him for helping to start the revolution. He was given a farcical trial and executed on December 30, 1896. This incited the people even more, and revolution broke out again and spread to the provinces of Pangasinan, Zambales, and Illocos.

By late 1897, Pedro Alejandro Paterno y de Ygnacio had successfully negotiated a cease fire, the famous Pact of Biak-na-Bato, between Aguinaldo and Fernando Primo de Rivera, the new governor-general. Primo de Rivera tried to stop the revolution by promising not to punish all rebels who surrendered peacefully to the government. Aguinaldo agreed that his men would turn in their arms and ammunition supplies. In return, Primo de Rivera would pay him the sum of 800,000 pesos in three equal installments. Also, Primo de Rivera would pay indemnities of 900,000 pesos to the families of noncombatant Filipinos who suffered grave losses during the war. Aguinaldo and his cadres went to Hong Kong in December carrying 400,000 pesos, the first installment of the promised 800,000 pesos. They did not completely trust the Spaniards and continued to organize and carried on the struggle. Meanwhile, the Spaniards reneged on their promise. Many of the revolutionaries who turned in their weapons were locked up, tortured, or even killed. Also, Primo de Rivera, having been apprised of Aguinaldo's activities in Hong Kong, never paid the rest of the installments.

THE REVOLUTION AGAINST THE UNITED STATES (1899–1902)

On April 25, 1898, war broke out between Spain and the United States after the destruction of the *Maine* in Havana Harbor, and the Americans accused Spain of sabotage. The American fleet under Commodore George Dewey, then at Hong Kong, received an order from the secretary of navy, John Long, to attack the Spanish at Manila. This offensive strategy had been planned several months before.[16] Dewey immediately cabled Aguinaldo with a pledge of America's support for the Filipino fight for independence, which inspired more Filipinos, especially in the provinces, to join the revolution.[17] Before Aguinaldo could reach Hong Kong from Singapore, however, Dewey had already left for Manila. After destroying the Spanish fleet at Cavite, he sent a ship to bring Aguinaldo and his companions to the Philippines. They arrived on May 19 and began gathering their forces against Spain.

Commodore Dewey easily defeated the poorly maintained and antiquated Spanish flotillas on May 1, 1898, but for some reason stalled for more than three months before taking control of the city (the official reason given was that he needed reinforcements). However, by the time the first American contingent arrived off Manila at the end of June, Aguinaldo's army had marched on Manila and consolidated their control of the city up to the shore of Manila Bay south of the capital. Manila was completely surrounded by the Filipinos when the Americans received the surrender of the Spanish troops, but the Filipinos were kept out of the city and prevented by the Americans from taking part in the surrender ceremonies. The Spanish authorities and the Americans had made a closed-door deal that the Filipinos would not be allowed to help take the surrender of the Spanish troops. The Americans believed that the surrender of Manila translated as the transfer of the country from Spain to the United States, but at the time, with the exception of Cavite, the rest of the country had already been liberated by the Filipino revolutionaries.

Relations between the Americans and the Filipinos began to deteriorate and continued to grow worse. The Filipinos realized that they had been betrayed by the Americans, and Aguinaldo's forces pushed rapidly to take over the whole country and establish a legitimate government outside of Manila. On June 12, 1898, the Filipino Revolutionary Congress proclaimed a provisional republic with Aguinaldo as the provisional president, and on September 19, 1898, moved the capital to Malolos. Aguinaldo's chief adviser, Apolinario Mabini, "the brains of the revolution," was charged with organizing the government. He wrote the laws that shaped the new government and that were intended to gain its recognition in the eyes of the international community. Mabini, who never trusted the Americans, warned the congressional assembly: "Let us not fool ourselves. The Americans, like the Spaniards and other European powers, covet this beautiful pearl of the Orient Seas, but we cherish its possession more, not only because God has given it to us, but because we have shed so much blood for its sake."[18] In November and December of that same year, 1898, revolutionary tribunals were also organized in the Visayas.

The first Philippine constitution and republic were approved by the Congress of the revolutionary government on November 29, 1898, and by Aguinaldo on December 23, who was elected president. Less than two weeks later, however, on the night of February 4, 1899, while President Aguinaldo was still in Malolos organizing the cabinet for the new republic, war broke out between Filipino and American troops in Manila. The Americans started the War of Philippine Independence when an American soldier named Private Robert W. Grayson shot and killed, without provocation, a Filipino soldier who was walking across the San Juan bridge.[19] Coincidentally, the following day, the U.S. Senate ratified the Treaty of Paris, by a very small margin, after a heated debate took place between the senators. Many Americans, at the time, were not in favor of colonizing the Philippines. The Anti-Imperialist League, led by notables like Mark Twain, was making fast headway convincing the public that colonization belied the traditions upon which the United States was founded and contradicted the very principles of the U.S. Constitution. Expansionist senators, mostly, from the industrializing northern states, however, saw the need for a refueling station in the Pacific and the Philippines as being strategically located near the Chinese markets. In contrast, the conservatives, predominantly from the southern states, opposed colonization because they considered the agrarian Philippines to be a competitor. This tension may have caused President William McKinley to announce a policy of "benevolent assimilation," which really meant that the United States would occupy and control the Philippine islands.

The Americans immediately sent enforcements to the Philippines, but they had underestimated the extent of the people's support for the revolutionary republic. Antonio Luna, the best trained military man among the Filipinos, was put in charge of military operations. Mabini as well as others wanted to have a strong leadership to confront the Americans. But, faced with the superior mechanical weapons and fighting power of the Americans, a split took place in the leadership of the revolution. One side favored independence and wanted to continue the struggle, those who followed Mabini and Luna. The other side argued for cessation of fighting and collaboration with the American colonizers so as to be in positions of influence and able to effect change. They followed Pedro Alejandro Paterno, the peace negotiator of the Biak-na-Bato and now president of the Malolos Congress, and Felipe Buencamino, an influential assemblyman. Mabini and Luna's opponents, who were mostly educated elite mestizos, assassinated Luna on June 5, 1899. With the downfall of Mabini and the death of Luna, the revolution faltered. On March 31, 1899, Malolos was captured by the Americans. Aguinaldo and his troops refused to surrender and, in November 1899, went underground to engage in guerilla warfare. He and his government were no longer secure in any one place from the pursuit of the American invaders. He was constantly on the move, and his men exhausted, ill fed, and poorly armed only with bolos and rifles. They often attacked the American troops at night. On March 23, 1901, Fredrick Funston aided by a group of Macabebe scouts from the Pampanga region, the latter of whom fought loyally for the Spanish regime and transferred their allegiance to the Americans, captured President Aguinaldo.[20]

William Howard Taft, who later became the first civil governor of the Philippines, officially proclaimed the end of the war, which the Americans falsely referred to as the insurrection. However, General Miguel Malvar continued to hold out in Samar until April 16, 1902, and his surrender marked the official end of the First Republic, though the Filipino struggle persisted. Most Filipinos resented and resisted the American occupation. After the Filipinos had for all practical purposes won their independence from Spain, by surrounding Manila on all fronts and gaining control over the rest of the country, Washington dispatched some 70,000 troops to pacify them, and the war that followed was one of the bloodiest colonial invasions in history. Historians often cite conflicting figures when discussing the casualties of this war, but according to the Philippine-American War Centennial Initiative, an organization charged with collecting accurate information, some 22,000 Philippine soldiers and 500,000 innocent civilians were killed between 1899 and 1902 in Luzon and the Visayas, while 100,000 Muslims were killed in Mindanao.[21] Also, the tragedies went beyond warfare by bringing in widespread famine and contagious diseases of poverty.

In summary, we have seen that local collective action against Spanish colonialism was manifested in a variety of nineteenth- and eighteenth-century protest movements and rebellions that culminated in the Philippine Revolution. The harsh reprisals of the Spanish against the nationalist intellectuals and secular clergy who called for reform incited the Filipinos to fight for freedom. Under General Emilio Aguinaldo, the Filipino army ousted Spain in 1898. Although U.S. Navy Admiral George Dewey sailed to the Philippines to help the patriots capture some 8,000 Spanish holed up in a garrison at Manila Bay, his doing so was not crucial to ending the Philippine war against Spain.[22] The Filipino army had surrounded and effectively closed off Manila and taken control of the whole country. However, the Americans prevented the Filipinos from entering Manila to participate in the surrender ceremonies. The United States had a self-interested motive for getting involved in the Filipino fight for independence. It wanted to expand its foreign market and trade for its manufactured goods and viewed the Philippines as a strategic stepping stone to the Chinese markets. So, soon after the nationalist victory over Spain, the archipelago was recolonized, this time by the United States, which sought to legitimate its claim by buying the islands from Spain at the signing of the treaty in Paris. The Filipino people fiercely resisted the American invasion, and colonization was forced upon them in 1901, although fighting continued intermittently and the nationalist struggle persisted.

NOTES

1. Herminia Menez, *Explorations in Philippine Folklore* (Manila: Ateneo de Manila Press, 1996), p. 86.

2. Cristina Blanc-Szanton, "Collision of Cultures: Historical Reformulation of Gender in the Lowland Visayas, Philippines," in *Power and Difference: Gender in Island Southeast Asia*, eds. Jane Atkinson and Shelly Errington (Stanford: Stanford University Press, 1990), pp. 345–83.

3. William Henry Scott, *Cracks in the Parchment Curtain and Other Essays in Philippine History* (Quezon City: New Day, 1982) and *Prehispanic Source Materials for the Study of Philippine History* (Quezon City: New Day, 1984).

4. H. de la Costa, *The Jesuits in the Philippines, 1581–1768* (Cambridge: Harvard University Press, 1961), pp. 314–315.

5. Herminia Menez, *Explorations in Philippine Folklore*, p. 93.

6. Sonia Zaide, "Filipino Revolts," in Sonia Zaide, *The Philippines, A Unique Nation* (Quezon City: All-Nations Publishing Company, 1999), pp. 179–202.

7. Sonia Zaide, *The Philippines, A Unique Nation*, p. 191.

8. James Putzel, *A Captive Land, The Politics of Agrarian Reform in the Philippines* (Manila: Ateneo de Manila University Press, 1992), p. 45.

9. James Putzel, *A Captive Land, The Politics of Agrarian Reform in the Philippines*, pp. 45–47.

10. Patricio Abinales and Donna Amoroso, *State and Society in the Philippines* (New York: Rowman and Littlefield Publishers, 2005), p. 69.

11. Thomas McKenna, *Muslims Rulers and Rebels: Everyday Politics and Armed Separatism in the Southern Philippines* (Berkeley: University of California Press, 1998).

12. *Noli me tangere* is Latin for "touch me not," an allusion to the gospel of St. John, in which Jesus says to Mary Magdelene, "Touch me not for I am not yet ascended to my Father." It continues to be one of the most influential political novels in the Philippine history and has inspired generations of Filipinos to struggle for a greater equity and justice. See Jose Rizal, *Noli Me Tangere, a Novel*, trans. Soledad Lacson-Locsin (Honolulu: University of Hawaii Press, 1966).

13. Mariano Apilado, *Revolutionary Spirituality: A Study of the Protestant Role in the American Colonial Rule of the Philippines, 1898–1928* (Quezon City: New Day, 1999), p. 20.

14. Andre Bonifacio lost battles in San Juan, Langka River, and Balara where he barely escaped with his life. This weakened his reputation as a military leader, which led to the rise General Aguinaldo, who became the official leader of the revolution. See Sonia Zaide, *The Philippines, A Unique Nation*, p. 239.

15. Sonia Zaide, *The Philippines, A Unique Nation*, p. 237.

16. Frank Hindan Golay, *Face of Empire, United States-Philippine Relations, 1898–1946* (Manila: Ateneo de Manila University Press, 1997), p. 19.

17. Aguinaldo and his companions approached Dewey earlier in Hong Kong with a proposal to conduct a joint offensive and defensive action against the Spanish. But Dewey had to await instructions from President McKinley. Meanwhile, Aguinaldo and his junta escaped to Singapore to avoid a lawsuit over the misuse of the reparation moneys paid by the Spanish. Aguinaldo needed to save the funds to use for the revolution. See Frank Hindan Golay, *Face of Empire, United States-Philippine Relations, 1898–1946*, p. 19.

18. Stephen Latorre, *Apolinario Mabini* (Manila: Tahan Books, 1992), p. 16.

19. Sonia Zaide, *The Philippines, A Unique Nation*, p. 268.

20. Mark Twain, who reported on location for the *New York Times*, documented the tactics used to capture President Aguinaldo: Lt. Colonel Funston put on a charade and had his Macabebe scouts dressed as revolutionary soldiers who pretended to be turning over captured American prisoners of war to Aguinaldo, whose camp was hidden deep in the mountainous interior of southern Luzon. Along the way, Funston and his men collapsed in hunger. He sent disguised scouts to get help from Aguinaldo, who sent back ample food to sustain them. After reaching camp, just as the Macabebes were about to turn over the POW to Aguinaldo, Funston hollered, "Macabebes, it's your turn," and the rest of the scouts who had surrounded them began shooting, and, in this way, President Aguinaldo was captured. Mark Twain argued that Funston broke a cardinal code because he attacked the hand that fed and saved him. See Mark Twain, "A Defense of General Funston," in *Mark Twain's Weapons of Satire, Anti-Imperialist Writings on the Philippine American War*, ed. Jim Zwick (New York: Syracuse University Press, 1992), pp. 124–130.

21. Patricio Abinales and Donna Amoroso, *State and Society in the Philippines*, p. 117.

22. Mark Twain, "Person Sitting in Darkness," in *Mark Twain's Weapons of Satire, Anti-Imperialist Writings on the Philippine American War*, p. 33.

4

American Colonization
(1899–1946)

The new colonizers continued to expand upon the traditional authority structure by working through wealthy landed elites to consolidate their colonial rule. In this way, they perpetuated and solidified the inequitable class system that was put in place by the Spanish and that continues to shape and characterize the Philippines in the twenty-first century, as we shall see in subsequent chapters.

THE COLONIZATION PROCESS

One month after the outbreak of the war, U.S. President William McKinley appointed Cornell University's President Jacob Gould Schurman to lead a mission to gather information about the Philippines and determine the nation's readiness for independence. They reported back to the president that the Filipinos were interested in gaining independence for their country. Still, the U.S. government proceeded to annex the Philippines at the signing of the Paris Peace Treaty in December 1898, and, then, it immediately dispatched reinforcements to pacify the islands.[1] McKinley ordered the American military government to take over the whole territory, using force if necessary. As a palliative to induce a quicker surrender, he emphasized that the United States had come "not as invaders or conquerors but as friends" to "civilize" and "Christianize" the Filipinos who had suffered long enough under the repressive Spanish.[2] What he didn't mention, however, was that the United States wanted to possess the Philippines to reach the markets and natural resources of Asia.

A few months later, on April 2, 1900, President McKinley dispatched a second Taft Commission with the instructions "to bear in mind that the government which they are establishing is designed not for our satisfaction nor for the expression of our theoretical views, but for the happiness, peace, and prosperity of the people of the Philippine islands, and the measures adopted should be made to conform with their customs, their habits and even their prejudices, to the fullest extent consistent with the accomplishment of the indispensable requisite of just and effective government."[3] While there was no explicit clause of independence in the instructions, the commissioners made such an allusion. They tried to convince the Filipinos that the U.S. government aimed to prepare them for eventual autonomy and self-rule. However, to use a Chinese proverb, "When the map unrolled, there was dagger," the commissioners emphasized that, given the superior might of the U.S. military, it would be foolish for them to oppose the new colonial order by setting up a republic of their own.

By the next year, McKinley was in the middle of his reelection campaign and wanted to create a better image of his colonial venture in the Philippines, especially with the rise of the opposition led by the anti-imperialist league, which was making great strides. So, he latched upon the idea that was recommended in the earlier commissioner's report of holding elections and establishing local governments in the Philippines.[4] McKinley appointed William Howard Taft as the first civil governor of the Philippines. He sent him with instructions to install municipal governments "in which the native of the islands shall be afforded the opportunity to manage their own local affairs to the fullest extent possible of which they were capable, and subject to the least degree of supervision and control which a careful study of their capacities and observations of the workings of native control show to be consistent with the maintenance of law, order, and loyalty."[5] The Taft commission had earlier also emphasized the need for building a public education system, with English as the language of instruction, and the infrastructure (roads, water supply, irrigation, hospitals, and hygiene) needed to make development possible. However, although the local governments law was intended to give the Filipinos more autonomy and self-government, in reality this was impossible to attain because the municipalities would all fall under the control and jurisdiction of the central government.

On July 4, 1901, Governor Taft inaugurated the first civil government in Manila and to him was transferred the executive powers that were formerly exercised by General Arthur MacArthur. Taft continued to serve as executive director of the Philippine Commission, which functioned as the legislative body. On September 1, 1901, Taft invited three prominent Filipinos, Dr. T. H. Pardo de Tavera, Benito Legarda Sr., and Jose Luzuriaga, to sit on this commission. These leaders used to support the Filipino revolution but resigned, early on, and joined the Americans. They were among the group of some 125 landed Filipinos who organized the Federalist Party on December 23, 1900, which promulgated for a peaceful compromise with the U.S. government of the military occupation. The Federalist Party was the only party encouraged by the early American colonial administrators.

Also, Taft initiated negotiations with the pope at Rome for the purchase of some 165,000 hectares (400,000 acres) of friar lands, which were finally bought on December 23, 1903, at a price of about $7,250,000. Governor Taft promised to credit the Philippine government for the amount, and bonds were issued. However, the U.S. authorities turned around and decided to sell the friar estates for the cost of purchase, which put it beyond the reach of the majority of Filipinos. Instead, it was the few wealthy *illustrados* and big landed elite families as well as at least one U.S. sugar corporation that "received the lion's share of the friars' estates."[6] The Taft Commission wanted to "redistribute" the land without incurring costs to the government, so this effectively precluded the possibility of implementing any real land reform.[7] For example, the commissioners passed a special law that exempted the friar lands from size limitations, which made it possible for the American Sugar Refining Corporation, also referred to as the Sugar Trust, to purchase the 22,000 hectare San Jose Estate in Mindoro. Another example was that the Tabacalera Company was able to expand its hacienda estate through the purchase of friar lands; it owned some 15,452 hectares by 1913. The pope also replaced the Spanish archbishop and bishops with U.S. bishops.

In 1904, Taft was called back to the U.S. mainland to become secretary of war, although he continued to direct Philippine affairs from Washington, D.C., even as his successor, Luke E. Wright, who had been a member of the Philippine Commission, became the new governor-general. In 1905, Taft took a party of senators and representatives to the islands, at the expense of the Philippine government, and on the eve of his presidential campaign on October 16, 1907, opened the legislature at Manila, although there was still fighting in the Visayas, and the act of 1902 required a state of "complete peace" before actually convening the legislature. Taft also inaugurated a massive program of organizing schools with the first teachers being American soldiers. Thousands of American teachers would later volunteer to serve in the Philippines. English was mandated as the language of instruction. Children studied the history of the United States, and they studied history as written from the perspective of Anglo-Americans. They were taught to look up to American culture and products as being superior to their own and were made to feel inferior to the "white" Americans. Meanwhile, Protestant missionaries taught the Filipinos how to read the Bible the way the Americans interpreted it, as being the foundation of the "God-given" American way of life, although, in reality, the Filipinos had their own private interpretations, and many continued to struggle for national independence.

COLONIAL REPRESSION OF THE NATIONALIST MOVEMENT

Even after Aguinaldo was captured in March of 1901, the nationalist revolutionaries did not waiver in their resistance, as the eye of the storm of war moved southward from the capital to the Visayas and Mindanao, which were engulfed in flames for at least another year. Even after General Miguel Malvar surrendered in April 1902, which marked the official end of the war, fighting persisted and continued to erupt sporadically, and small acts of resistance occurred, routinely. For example, Apolinario Mabini,[8] among others, went into exile in Guam rather than take the oath of allegiance to the United States. Small peasants already frustrated and disabused by unfair landlord practices gave safe harbor to their revolutionary countrymen and countrywomen. The U.S. military brutally retaliated against those who resisted, and, indeed, the Filipinos were forced to surrender because they rejected and resisted the American colonial project.

In the aftermath of war, the conditions in the Philippines were devastating. Filipinos suffered severely from epidemics, poverty, famines, droughts, and loss of family members. Also, the cost for the United States was high. Reports show that 4,234 American soldiers died in action and 2,818 were wounded, and thousands more contracted life-threatening diseases in the islands. It cost the United States some $600 million [the equivalent of about US$4 billion in 1989], and additional millions were spent on benefits and pensions.[9]

The propaganda used by the Americans to justify their colonial design was greatly "contradicted by her conduct in the Philippines." The U.S. military killed more Filipinos in 3 years than the Spanish killed in 300 years.[10] While McKinley was criticizing the Spanish policy of *reconcentrados* as being barbaric and uncivilized, the U.S. government adopted the same practices. The U.S. military tortured civilians, massacred local populations, and burned down towns, among other atrocities. One such town in Samar was razed to the ground and its inhabitants massacred by U.S. forces, as described in the following passage:

the Americans were dismayed to discover that Aguinaldo's capture and surrender appeal made no perceptible difference in the fighting, which continued unabated. This was too much for MacArthur, who resigned and was replaced by Major General Adna Chaffee.

By mid-summer 1901, the focus of war started to shift south of Manila. Some of the guerilla leaders in northern and Central Luzon who were close to Aguinaldo began to surrender. Others held out, however, and General Miguel Malvar, operating in Batangas, was proving to be every bit as difficult for the Americans as Aguinaldo had been...

On the eve of the Samar campaign, the war was clearly degenerating into mass slaughter. It was hardly precise to call it "war" any longer. The Americans were simply chasing ragged, poorly armed bands of guerillas and, failing to catch them, were inflicting severe punishment on those they could catch—the people of the villages and barrios in the theater of operation.

In late September, in the town of Balangiga, Samar, American troops had for some time been abusing the townspeople by packing them into open wooden pens at night where they were forced to sleep standing in the rain. Several score of guerilla General Vincent Lukban's bolomen infiltrated the town and on the morning of September 28, while the Americans were eating their breakfast, Lukban's men suddenly fell upon them. Heads dropped into breakfast dishes. Fifty-four Americans were boloed to death, and few of the eighteen survivors escaped serious injury.

The Balangiga massacre issued a reign of terror the likes of which had not been seen in this war. General ["Howling Jake"] Smith, fresh from his victories in northern Luzon and Panay, was chosen to lead the American mission of revenge. Smith's order to his men embarking on the Samar campaign could not have been more explicit: "Kill and burn, kill and burn, the more you kill and the more you burn the more you please me." It was, said Smith, "no time to take prisoners." War was to be waged "in the sharpest and most decisive manner possible." When asked to define the age limit for killing, Smith gave his infamous reply: "Everything over ten." Smith ordered Samar to be turned into a "howling wilderness" so that "even the birds could not live there." It was boasted that...what fire and water (e.g., water torture)...had done in Panay, water and fire would do to Samar." The now-familiar pattern of operations began once again. All inhabitants of the island (pop. 266,000) were ordered to present themselves to detention camps in several of the larger coastal towns. Those who did not (or those who did not make it their business to learn of the existence of the order); and were found outside the detention camp perimeter, would be shot," and no questions asked." Few reporters covered the carnage; one who did noted..."During my stay in Samar the only prisoners that were made...were taken by Waller's command; and I heard this act criticized by the highest officers as a mistake...The truth is, the struggle in Samar is one of extermination."

In the face of mounting and irrefutable evidence of the true conduct of the war, the War Department resorted to by-now-standard procedure—deny, minimize, obliterate charges and criticisms with a blizzard of rhetorical overkill. Secretary Root: "the warfare has been conducted with the marked humanity and magnanimity on the part of the U.S."[11]

While General Smith was preoccupied in Samar, Major General Chaffee assigned Brigadier General Franklin Bell to conduct operations against the underground resistance in southern Luzon. Bell ran concentration camps without providing adequate food, medicines, or supplies. He issued a proclamation that "anyone who is not a friend is an enemy." It was a horrific time for Filipinos, and it was difficult to know how one could become a friend to the Americans.

> By guiding troops to camps of the enemy, by publicly identifying "insurgents," by accompanying troops in their operations against the guerillas, by denouncing the "enemy" publicly, and by identifying secret guerilla supporters. Those who were suspected of aiding and abetting the revolution for independence could be arrested, imprisoned, and even tortured, without evidence or making public the charges against them.[12]

When Mark Twain and others reported in the U.S. press about these massacres, an uproar arose in the country, and the U.S. Congress called for an investigation. But, the three generals (Smith, Bell, and Chaffee) were eventually exonerated by the U.S. Congress and soon were promoted to the rank of senior generals of the U.S. Army.[13]

Finally, on April 2, 1902, the last Filipino general, Miguel Malvar, surrendered at Batangas, although many of his men refused to give up and continued fighting off and on in the provinces and elsewhere in the country. On July 4, President Roosevelt, officially, announced the end of the war and made the Philippines a U.S. colony.

THE COLONIAL RULE

In the years following the Philippine-American War, the U.S. government consolidated its political control and governance over the colony. It expanded upon the Spanish legal system by adding some new laws such as the Civil Marriage Code and Philippine Bill of 1902, which included provisions for (1) the extension of the Bill of Rights to the Filipino people, except the right to a jury trial; (2) appointment of two Filipino resident commissioners in Washington, D.C.; (3) establishment of an elective Philippine assembly, after the proclamation of complete peace and two years after the published census; (4) the retention of the Philippine Commission as the upper house of the legislature, with the Philippine assembly acting as the lower house; and (5) the conservation of the natural resources of the Philippines for the Filipinos.[14]

In accordance with the Philippine Commission's instructions to encourage Filipinos to enter government, Gregorio Araneta was appointed in 1899, as the first chief justice of the Supreme Court, as well as the secretary of finance.[15] By 1912, half the judges on the Supreme Court were Filipinos; by 1926, only two out of the 55 judges were Americans.[16] In 1907, after the municipal government structures were instituted, elections were held for the National Assembly that would serve as the elective lower house of the legislature with the Philippine Commission as the appointed upper house, and the governor-general as the executive director. Only males 21 years of age and older who had resided six months in the district and had held either local office prior to August 13, 1898, owned real property to the value of 500 pesos, or who could read, speak, and write either English or Spanish were eligible to vote. According to U.S. War Department statistics, over 100,000 registered to vote for the assembly elections, and of those, 94 percent voted."[17] Significantly, the results of this election show that the Filipinos were motivated by their desire for independence. Fifty-eight of the 80 members elected to sit on this assembly belonged to the Nationalist Party, which advocated for immediate independence. Sergio Osmena Sr. from Cebu was nominated by Manuel Quezon and elected as the Speaker, which was the highest political office available to a Filipino, and second only to the governor-general. Manuel Quezon from Tayabas was elected the majority floor leader. Osmena served as Speaker of the Philippine assembly until Quezon was elected in 1922.

Philippine politics became one-party politics, since the majority of the politicians, with the exception of Manuel Quezon[18] who rose to prominence through his academic merit, were from the wealthy upper class. To keep the loyalty of their constituents they had to be for independence, so the political leaders (e.g., Osmena versus Quezon) who struggled with each other to control the assembly had no real ideological differences. One explanation is that "affiliation was based on affinities of blood, friendship, and regionalism, as well as on personal expedience. Under these circumstances, patronage was vital to the retention of a personal following, a fact which induced the party leaders time and time again to barter the country's long-range interests for short-term bonuses for the party of power."[19] For example, in 1909, the Filipino assembly rightly opposed the Payne Aldrich Bill, which provided for free trade, because it would make the Philippines dependent on the United States. However, after Governor-General James Smith, who served from 1906 to 1909, and Vice Governor Forbes, who later became governor from 1909 to 1913, held a private conference with Quezon, the assembly leaders privately declared this bill would be good for Filipinos. Most of the issues that the Filipino assembly voted on were decided on the basis of "personalism" and family alliances. Also, the Filipino politicians for pragmatic reasons had to retain the goodwill of the commission and governor-general.

In 1913, when the Democratic Party won the presidency in the United States, American policy shifted in favor of Philippine independence. Francis B. Harrison of New York succeeded as governor-general who served from 1913 to 1921, the longest tenure of any U.S. governor-general. He earned the trust and loyalty of the Filipinos for his Filipinization policy, which was opposed by American businesses and the retired army community that settled in the country. He appointed five Filipinos to a nine-member Philippine Commission, which served in the upper house of the legislature from 1907 to 1906; in the lower house, the Philippine assembly was all-Filipino. In 1916, he implemented the Jones Law for an elective Philippine Senate, except two senators who represented the non-Christians were appointed by the governor-general. All measures passed by the Philippine legislature had to be reported to the U.S. Congress, which had the power to annul them, and the governor-general retained supreme executive power. The Jones law also provided a constitution and declared the intention of the United States to recognize Philippine independence as soon as a stable government could be established.

However, when the Republicans resumed power they criticized Harrison's Filipinization policy. Critics contended that the governor-general's office had been weakened, first, by reducing the American presence in the civil service and in the executive department and, second, by consulting with the Filipino leaders. When Harrison took office in 1913, there were 2,680 Americans in all branches of government; in 1919, the number was reduced to 614. Meanwhile, Filipinos increased from 6,033 in 1912 to 13,240 in 1921. The incoming President Harding immediately dispatched the Wood-Forbes mission to investigate the Philippine question. Forbes reported back that the granting of independence would be premature and urged the U.S. government not be left in a position of responsibility without authority. Wood, who had served as a former major general in the regular army and the military governor of Cuba and, later, of the Philippine Muslim area in Mindanao, was appointed the new governor-general of the Philippines in October 1921. He served mostly through undersecretaries for the next six years, until 1927, when he died in Boston. His administration was characterized as being repressive and systematic in its assertion of American authority. Wood's policies and activities were looked upon favorably by the American business community in Manila, which were intended to stabilize and increase business, but the Filipinos saw them as being regressive and undoing of all the progress that was made toward self-government. His authoritarian and top-down style had the reverse effect of strengthening Filipino adversity and resistance against the colonial regime.

Under successive governor-generalships of Henry Stimson (1928–1929), Dwight Davis (1929–1932), and Theodore Roosevelt (1932–1933), the controversy between those for and against independence reached a climax. The Filipino leaders established information centers in Washington, D.C., and Manila

to disseminate and provide accurate information on the Philippines. They lobbied the U.S. Congress, while pro-independence delegations traveled across
the United States on speaking tours to increase public awareness. On June 15,
1933, President F. D. Roosevelt appointed a pro-independence advocate, Frank
Murphy of Michigan as governor-general, who served until 1936. But, his successor, Paul McNutt of Indiana (1936–1939), who recognized the value of the
islands as a source for cheap tropical products and mineral wealth, argued
against granting independence but it was too late to change the U.S. policy.
Francis B. Sayer, a former faculty member of Harvard University and later secretary of state, was appointed the new governor-general on October 21, 1939.
His assignment was to prepare the Philippines for independence.

For as early as 1929, the Filipino campaign for independence gained new allies in the United States, including dairy farmers, farm organizations, domestic
sugar producers, cordage manufacturers, tobacco producers, and producers of
hydrogenated fats and other products and labor unions which feared the competition of Filipino immigrants. A bill supporting these interests and providing
for independence finally passed both houses of congress, was vetoed by President Hoover, but passed again over the veto in January 1933. However, this
bill failed to be ratified by the Philippine legislature because of the opposition
of Manuel Quezon, while both Sergio Osmena and Manuel Roxas were in favor
of it. Quezon was able to pass a resolution against the measure in the Philippine legislature in October 1933, which listed four main objections: the trade
provisions; the immigration restrictions; the allocation of indefinite powers to
the high commissioner; and the military and naval restrictions, which were
considered to be "inconsistent with true independence."[20]

President Franklin Roosevelt who took office in March 1933, approved the
bill on the condition that the provision reserving for permanent military bases,
except for naval stations, be eliminated. The Tydings-McDuffe Act, also known
as the Philippine Independence Act, was enacted into law on March 24, 1934,
and the 10-year Philippine commonwealth was established with independence
scheduled for 1946. The Filipinos accepted the Tydings-McDuff Act primarily
because they thought that it was the best compromise that they could secure
at the time and it was implied that there would be a later review.[21] The act provided for a continuation of trade relations with a graduate tax on Philippine
exports to the United States of 5 percent of the corresponding duty for the first
year, and increasing by 5 percent for each subsequent year. This was amended
by the act of 1939 that exempted cigars, tobacco, coconut oil, and pearl or shell
buttons, which were added to the free quota list (that already listed hemp and
copra) reducible by 5 percent each year. The U.S. immigration laws were applied and limited the annual Filipino quota to 50.

In the resulting Philippine commonwealth constitution, the presidency, vice
presidency, and existing unicameral National Assembly was retained but the

single six-year term for the president and single chamber legislature were eliminated by amendments adopted in 1939, and approved by President Roosevelt on March 23 and ratified that same year by popular vote. On November 4, 1941, President Quezon, who had already served for six years, was reelected for another four years. During his tenure, there was widespread social and political unrest as labor unions and radical peasant organizations agitated for land reform and greater economic justice. The Philippine army, which had been trained under the supervision of Douglas MacArthur, the son of the last military general in the Philippines, was called into active service by the U.S. government to fight against the Japanese invasion on December 8, 1941.

THE JAPANESE OCCUPATION

On December 8, 1941, the Japanese launched an air raid and bombed the joint U.S.–Philippine military installations in the islands, within hours of its attack on Pearl Harbor. The poorly equipped Filipino and American forces were no match for the superior forces of the Japanese, although they put up a brave resistance, until they had to withdraw in accordance with a prearranged plan to the Bataan peninsula. General Douglas MacArthur was ordered by President Roosevelt to retreat to Australia, although he vowed to return to liberate the Philippines. President Quezon, Vice President Osmena and a few others were evacuated by the Americans and the Philippine government was established in exile in the United States. It is interesting to note that General Brigadier Manuel Roxas (who became the last president of the Philippine commonwealth and, then, first president of the republic) refused to leave with Quezon; he thought that he could do more good if he stayed behind with his people and troops.[22] The remaining U.S.–Philippine forces knew that no more reinforcements or supplies would come from the United States, and that all available material was being sent to Europe. On April 9, 1942, General Edward P. King had no other choice than to surrender "to stop the killing of more helpless defenders,"[23] who were already doomed and ravaged with diseases and hunger at Bataan. It is noted that "more than 76,000 United States Armed Forces of the Far East (USAFFE) forces, including 66,000 Filipinos laid down their arms. Aside from these prisoners of war., there were an estimated 26,000 civilian refugees who were trapped behind the USAFFE lines in Bataan."[24] The last contingent fought valiantly against the onslaught of thousands of Japanese infantrymen and under constant shelling from sea and air, from deep within the tunnels of Corregidor. On May 6, 1942, the surrender at Corregidor of General Wainwright marked the end of the military's resistance, although some forces escaped and guerilla units continued to resist the Japanese from the outskirts. Even though the war was declared to be over for the American forces in the Philippines, the Filipinos continued to organize themselves into guerilla units and resistance movements against the Japanese throughout the duration of World War II.

The Japanese used false rhetoric to justify their taking control of the Philippines. Marching under the slogan of "Asians for Asians," they announced that they had come in solidarity with the people of Asia to liberate them from colonialism. Like the Americans, the Japanese allowed the Filipinos to operate the government but under much closer scrutiny and supervision. In 1943, Japan held an independence ceremony to inaugurate the Second Republic of the Philippines, but it was a puppet government and the Japanese government pulled the strings. Yet, it is important to remember that "this interregnum also served to turn the kaleidoscope, altering perceptions on collaboration, resistance, and allowing nationalists visions to reemerge. Regionally, the Japanese invasion of Southeast Asia marked the beginning of the end of Western rule"[25] and gave new impetus to anti-Japanese, anticolonial, and nationalist movements in their struggle for liberation.

PEASANT RESISTANCE MOVEMENTS

The Japanese occupation lasted from January 2, 1942, to February 1945. During this time, many landowners and provincial governing officials moved to the cities, especially Manila, and collaborated with the Japanese to protect their own assets. Meanwhile, tenant farmers and peasants who had already been opposing unfair landlord practices, took back the land, joined guerilla units, and prevented the Japanese from entering their territories. One of the largest of these resistance movements was the Hukbong Bayan laban sa Hapon or Hukbalahap (People's Army Against the Japanese), which was the most highly effective underground unit in central Luzon, during the Japanese occupation. Between 1943 and 1944, this unit had an estimated 70,000 guerillas and hundreds of thousands of supporters throughout the country.[26] It cooperated closely with the U.S. Army in the liberation campaign but, after the war, the HUK became an "object" of repression as it was branded a "Communist" front. However, the so-called Communists joined forces with the anti-Fascist alliance against Japan during World War II. When the war was over, they took up the cause of the peasants, while the Filipino landed elites wanted to reinstate the traditional power structure by restoring the old landlord-to-tenant system.

In other words, by the time the Americans returned to the Philippines, the HUK had already liberated most of Cagayan from the Japanese occupation army. At the final stages of the war against the Japanese, the HUK guerrillas fought along with the American forces until the Japanese were completely defeated. After the war, however, when most of the guerilla organizations were being recognized for their services to the American cause, many of the HUK guerillas were being arrested, forcibly disarmed, and thrown into jail without any charges by the U.S. Army. The Americans justified their actions on the grounds that the HUKs were not members of the USAFFE, and their leaders, as alleged by the U.S. military intelligence officers, were communists and socialists.[27] The Filipino military police and civilian guards massacred HUK members and civilians believed to be supporters of the HUK movement often with the knowledge of American military officers.[28] Knowing that their former allies were after them, the majority of the HUKs went underground waging a guerilla war against the government, specifically against the American counter-intelligence corps (CIA), the Filipino military police, and the civilian guards. The civilian guards composed mostly of USAFFE guerillas and private guards of wealthy landlords, were under the discrete command of military commanders who provided them with guns to fight the HUKs.[29] The HUK resistance movement evolved out of earlier uprisings and acts of resistance against the unequal landowning system and repression of the U.S.–Philippine colonial government.

The HUK Army grew out of earlier twentieth-century peasant reactions against the American colonization of northern and central Luzon.[30] At that time, Ilocano homesteaders populated the scattered farm communities of Cagayan Valley in central Luzon as a result of the American colonial "land reform" policy. Their ancestral villages along the northern coast were becoming overcrowded and increasingly impoverished. Hence, poor farmers and fishers, especially disinherited sons, were pushed from their home regions to Cagayan Valley, Mindanao, and the United States in search of economic opportunities. Other landlords would sell, or mortgage, their land to send their children to school in hopes of launching them into politically powerful careers. Cagayan Valley was initially inhabited by the Ibanags, who were the original farmers along the Cagayan River, and Kalingas from surrounding mountains and plains were pushed out by the American colonial regime to prepare the way for the coming of the Ilocanos.[31] Initially, the American colonizers purchased large friar estates then sold them again piecemeal to a few Filipino oligarchies and U.S. corporations. Then, indigenous farms and swiddens not being cultivated in Cagayan Valley were taken from the Kalingas, Ibanags, and Gaddangs by the Ilocanos who were granted, or sold, homesteads in the area by the colonial government. In this manner, the American colonial regime helped to initiate the production of cash cropping to promote agricultural development in the valley.[32]

The American colonial process worked directly through local landed elites and officials to promote the interests of American businesses. The empowerment of prominent Filipinos was shaped as much by colonial design as it was made in reaction to local resistance movements. It provided economic and political elite families and politicians with additional power and authority. Hence, landlords could change the terms of agreement between themselves and their peasants, and they could relinquish their pledge to provide social security to those who worked the land. In time, peasants became transformed into tenants and wageworkers who shared similar working conditions, and who began to organize for their own interests.

This change dynamic can be reillustrated with a final example. Some of the tactics used by the American colonial and Chinese mestizo sugar barons on Negros Island in the central Visayas to acquire their workers were "forced expropriation of peasant farms later legitimized by legal documentation: cash purchase of small peasant farms to form a plantation: and high interest loans to peasant proprietors with default provisions requiring forfeiture of land and years of debt bondage."[33] Once the land was cleared, sugar overlords used similar strategies to maintain their workforce: they imported migrant laborers from Panay (e.g., dispossessed textile workers who lost their jobs when colonial entrepreneurs flooded the local market with cheap cloth produced in Britain and the American northeast, as a result of the Industrial Revolution) and bought off permanent migrants with cash advances and indebted them with high interest loans when they arrived. However, these tactics were not enough to keep their workers intact. Plantation owners used violence, corporeal punishment, and military guards to prevent workers from escaping.

Plantation owners began to ship sugar off the coast of Negros only after stevedores on the nearby island of Iloilo protested against them, and demonstrated that they could no longer be repressed. The dockworkers demanded better wages and working conditions from their employers, and were defeated only after the steam engine, which permitted the shipment of sugar from Negros, was invented.

The plantation workers on Negros, also, organized themselves to demonstrate against their owners. Their efforts were less successful than the stevedores of Iloilo because the workforces of Negros were stratified and divided among themselves as a class by the conditions under which they labored. The plantations of Negros were "tightly run factories" in the field. They were administered by sugar lords who hired supervisors from their workers to coerce "debt slaves who owned nothing more than their clothes and their cooking utensils" to work for them.[34] The internal peasant class on the plantation became a stratified class but it remained a single class in relation to other classes in the wider society. Plantation owners did not hesitate to crush emerging labor unions by using military force and infiltrating them with their henchmen. Meanwhile, as we will see in chapter six, the sugar workers continued to resist into the twenty-first century.

LIBERATION OF THE ISLANDS

Late 1944, the tides of war turned as General Douglas MacArthur's island-hopping strategy gained new strategic victories for the allied forces against

Japan. From August to October 1944, the United States was winning the war in the Pacific as American planes began bombing targets in the Philippines.[35] On October 20, 1944, General MacArthur with his amphibious forces of some 174,000 troops landed on Leyte in the central Philippines. He was accompanied by President Osmena,[36] General Carlos Romulo, and General Basilio Valdez, who reinstated the commonwealth government.

General MacArthur's forces met with fierce almost fanatical resistance, as Lieutenant General Tomoyuki Yamashita ordered reinforcements to Leyte by sea and air. The Americans equipped with new smaller more powerful rifles, flame-throwers, amphibian tanks, and faster fighter planes attacked the Japanese on all sides. The Japanese reacted with desperation as suicide bombers known as kamikazes crashed into American planes and warships in Leyte Gulf. Meanwhile, three columns of Japanese navy fleets were racing towards Leyte. Japan's central fleet was coming in from Singapore, the southern fleet was approaching upward from Borneo, and the northern column was descending down from Formosa (Taiwan). These three columns were intercepted by the American navy under Rear Admiral J. B. Oldendorf, Admiral William Halsey, and Rear Admiral Thomas Sprague, which annihilated them. This critical defeat of the Japanese navy paved the way for the liberation of the Philippines.

By December 1944, the Japanese evacuated President Laurel and his cabinet to Baguio, as their forces began to retreat to a battle line running northward from Anitpolo to Appari. In their retreat, they pillaged Filipino homes, tortured and massacred innocent civilians, and burned towns and villages.[37] Meanwhile, on February 5, 1945, MacArthur's forces set a course for the capital region to entrap the Japanese troops based in southern Manila. Reacting in crazed desperation, the Japanese plunged Ermita Malate and Intramuros into a bloodied den of horror. They pillaged, raped, and murdered innocent civilians and religious clergy. They burned to the ground historic districts of homes, government buildings, universities, libraries, and churches. MacArthur's troops penetrated the capital region from the north, on February 7, engaged in bloody combat, and retook Manila on February 23, 1945. Over the course of this month-long battle, 1,000 American soldiers, 16,000 Japanese soldiers, and tens of thousands Filipinos lost their lives. Eighty percent of Manila was demolished, making it the most devastated city in the war, after Warsaw.[38]

On February 27, 1945, the Americans transferred the powers of government to President Osmena. No military government was formerly instituted even for the interim period, but the commonwealth government was still dependent on the American military for all of the facilities essential to governance. As we shall see in the next chapter, although the American military government was not instituted in the Philippines, it still exerted a formative influence over Philippine political affairs.

NOTES

1. David Wurfel, "The Philippines" in *Governments and Politics of Southeast Asia*, ed. George McTurnan Kahin (Ithaca: Cornell University Press, 1964), p. 686.

2. Excerpt from Frank Hindman Golay, *Face of Empire, United States-Philippine Relations 1898–1946* (Manila: Ateneo de Manila Press, 1997), pp. 47–90.

3. Excerpt from David Wurfel, "The Philippines," in *Governments and Politics of Southeast Asia*, p. 686; full text in Appendix III of Dean Worcester, *The Philippines, Past and Present* (New York: Macmillan, 1930).

4. Stuart Creighton Miller, *Benevolent Assimilation: The American Conquest of the Philippines 1899–1903* (New Haven: Yale University Press, 1982), p. 133.

5. Jean Grossholtz, *Politics in the Philippines* (Boston: Little Brown and Company, 1964), p. 24.

6. James Putzel, *A Captive Land: The Politics of Agrarian Reform in the Philippines* (Manila: Ateneo de Manila Press, 1992), p. 53.

7. James Putzel, *A Captive Land*, p. 53.

8. Readers interested in a first-hand account are referred to Apolinario Mabini, *The Philippine Revolution (With Other Documents of the Period)*, Vol. II (Manila: The National Historical Institute, n.d.).

9. Stanley Karnow, *In Our Image, America's Empire in the Philippines* (New York: Ballantine Books, 1989), p. 194.

10. Thomas Schoonover, *Uncle Sam's War of 1898 and the Origins of Globalization* (Lexington: The University of Kentucky Press, 2003), pp. 95–96.

11. Luzviminda Francisco, "The First Vietnam: The Philippine-American War, 1899–1902," in *The Philippines Reader, A History of Colonialism, NeoColonialism, and Dictatorship and Resistance*, eds. Daniel B. Schirmer and Stephen Rosskamm Shalom (Boston: Southend Press, 1978), pp. 16–17.

12. Luzviminda Francisco, "The First Vietnam: The Philippine-American War, 1899–1902," in *The Philippines Reader, A History of Colonialism, NeoColonialism, and Dictatorship and Resistance*, eds. Schirmer and Shalom, p. 18.

13. Thomas Schoonover, *Uncle Sam's War of 1898 and the Origins of Globalization*, p. 93.

14. Sonia Zaide, *The Philippines, A Unique Nation* (Manila: All Nations Publishing Co., 1999), p. 283.

15. Sonia Zaide, *The Philippines, A Unique Nation*, p. 282.

16. David Wurfel, "The Philippines," in *Governments and Politics of Southeast Asia*, ed. George McTurnan Kahin, p. 687.

17. Jean Grossholtz, *Politics in the Philippines*, p. 25.

18. Manuel Quezon was born in 1878 of humble teachers in Baler, a small village on the east coast of Luzon. As a young man, he worked his way through law school as a houseboy in a friar rectory. Although his studies were interrupted when he joined the revolution, after the war, he completed his degree

and served his country. He has been referred to as the "Father of Philippine Independence." For details, see Carlos Quirino, *Manuel L. Quezon* (Manila: Tahanan Books, 1995).

19. Renato Constantino, *The Philippines, A Past Revisited,* Vol. 1 (Quezon City: Renato Constantino, 1975; 16th printing, 1998), pp. 325–326.

20. Shirley Jenkins, "The Independence Lobby," in *The Philippines Reader, A History of Colonialism, NeoColonialism, and Dictatorship and Resistance,* eds. Daniel B. Schirmer and Stephen Rosskamm Shalom, p. 57.

21. Shirley Jenkins, "The Independence Lobby," in *The Philippines Reader, A History of Colonialism, NeoColonialism, and Dictatorship and Resistance,* eds. Daniel B. Schirmer and Stephen Rosskamm Shalom, p. 57.

22. General Roxas was later captured by the Japanese in Mindanao on May 11, 1942, and was ordered by General Yoshihide Hayashi to be executed for refusing to collaborate with the Japanese. But a Christian Japanese officer, Lt. Col. Nobuhiko Jimbo, intervened and saved his life; see Sonia Zaide, *The Philippines, A Unique Nation,* p. 333.

23. Sonia Zaide, *The Philippines, A Unique Nation,* p. 330.

24. Sonia Zaide, *The Philippines, A Unique Nation,* p. 330.

25. Patricio Abinales and Donna Amoroso, *State and Society in the Philippines* (New York: Rowman & Littlefield Publishers, 2005), p. 160.

26. Amy Blitz, *The Contested State, American Foreign Policy and Regime Change in the Philippines* (New York: Rowman & Littlefield, 2000), p. 70

27. Bendict Kerkvliet, *The Huk Rebellion: A Study of Peasant Revolt in the Philippines* (Berkeley: University of California Press, 1977), pp. 145, 147.

28. Teodoro Agoncillo and Milagros Guerrero, *History of the Filipino People* (Quezon City: Garcia Publishing House, 1984), pp. 524–525.

29. Teodoro Agoncillo and Milagros Guerrero, *History of the Filipino People;* Bendict Kerkvliet, *The Huk Rebellion: A Study of Peasant Revolt in the Philippines;* Ecumenical Movement for Justice and Peace, *Primer on Militarization* (Manila: The Ecumenical Movement for Justice and Peace, 1988).

30. Bendict Kerkvliet, *The Huk Rebellion: A Study of Peasant Revolt in the Philippines.*

31. Eugene Verstraelen, SVD, Ph.D., personal communication in Kathleen Nadeau, *A Content Analysis of Ibanag Proverbs,* M.A. Thesis (Cebu City: University of San Carlos, 1980), p. 30.

32. Akira Takahashi, *Land and Peasants in Central Luzon, Socio-Economic Structure of a Philippine Village* (Honolulu: East-West Center, 1969); Henry Lewis, *Illocano Rice Farmers: A Comparative Study of Two Philippine Barrios* (Honolulu: University of Hawaii Press, 1971).

33. Alfred McCoy, "A Queen Dies Slowly: The Rise and Fall of Iloilo City," in *Local Trade and Global Transformations,* ed. Alfred McCoy (Honolulu: University of Hawaii Press, 1982), pp. 320–321.

34. Alfred McCoy, "A Queen Dies Slowly: The Rise and Fall of Iloilo City," in *Local Trade and Global Transformations*, ed. Alfred McCoy, p. 325.

35. Sonia Zaide, *The Philippines, A Unique Nation*, p. 349

36. Manuel Quezon (1878–1944), who served as president of the Philippine commonwealth government in exile, died in the United States on August 1, 1944.

37. Sonia Zaide, *The Philippines, A Unique Nation*, p. 350.

38. Patricio Abinales and Donna Amoroso, *State and Society in the Philippines*, p. 163.

5

Philippine Independence (Post–World War II)

By the end of the war, President Quezon had already died in exile in August 1944 and was succeeded by Vice President Osmena, who assumed the office of president of the commonwealth government. He was charged with the task of reestablishing the constitutional government in Manila, while dealing with those who had collaborated with the Japanese. This was a difficult position because the president had to reconstitute the legislature, when a large proportion of those who served in both Houses had collaborated with the Japanese. To complicate matters, General MacArthur had already breached the American policy on collaborators, which required their removal from public office, by granting clemency and liberating his friends and business partners who had collaborated with the Japanese. This meant that those who had collaborated with the Japanese were those who were charged with the task of dealing with the problem of collaborators, which, effectively, ensured the survival of the prewar landed elites. In this chapter, we will look at some of the challenges and opportunities that confronted the newly independent Republic of the Philippines under the first five postwar presidents: Manual Roxas, Elpidio Quirino, Ramon Magsaysay, Carlos Garcia, and Diosdado Macapagal.

FROM COMMONWEALTH TO REPUBLIC

On July 4, 1945, the U.S. government granted the Philippines independence in accordance with a long-standing agreement and, partly, as a result of pressure from U.S. domestic and economic interests. Most of the infrastructure in the country had been demolished. Manila was completely in shambles and devastated by the war. Housing, schools, medicines, food, and supplies were desperately needed. The cost of living had skyrocketed as much as 800 percent higher than before the war. Responding to this urgent need for aid, in 1945, governmental arrangements were made to transfer $71,500,000 to the Philippines, which had accumulated in the United States as excise taxes collected on Philippine coconut oil imports, and to return $6 million in securities that had been deposited by the Philippine government before the war as surety for military equipment. These funds were supplemented by a loan of $75 million from the United States Reconstruction Finance Corporation in mid-1946.[1]

President Osmena, who became president after Quezon had died in the United States in August of 1944, returned with General Douglas MacArthur to the Philippines. The civil government was restored, but the military ran the country, at least for the next several months. Osmena wanted MacArthur to clarify the issue of collaboration, but this question strained their relationship. MacArthur sabotaged Osmena's attempts to prosecute collaborators: "The most dramatic was MacArthur's 'liberation' in April of 1945 of his prewar friend Manuel Roxas, who had been minister without portfolio in Laurel's cabinet and director of the wartime rice procurement agency which supplied the Japanese army."[2] Then, Roxas became the political leader of the newly reinstalled Philippine Congress. That same year, President Osmena won the presidential nomination of the Nationalista Party, but Roxas refused to give way and formed a new liberal party wing, which eventually became the Liberal Party, so that he could run for president.[3] So President Osmena formed an alliance between the Nationalistas and the Democratic front, which included members of the middle classes and many of the organized peasant movements, including the HUKs of northern and central Luzon. While Osmena tended to his administrative duties in Manila and allowed the electoral process to work, Roxas campaigned around the country, spending large sums of money. He had three main campaign issues: first, he argued that those who had collaborated with the Japanese also resisted; second, he promised to "save" the country from the so-called Communist threat (meaning the HUK rebels who had fought against the Japanese during World War II and now wanted land reform); third, he argued that he would adopt new economic policies that would bring the Philippines into a new era.

Roxas won by 200,000 votes, and gained control of both houses of Congress. One of the first acts passed under his administration was the notorious Bell

Trade Act. The Bell Trade Act of 1946, also referred to as the Philippine Trade Act, allowed free trade for eight years and diminishing tariff preferences for 20 years thereafter. One of the most controversial items in this bill was the parity clause, which stated that "the exploitation and development of natural resources and lands in the public domain and the operations of public utilities shall if open to any person, be open to citizens of the United States."[4] In addition, there was a clause in the Rehabilitation Act that required the Philippine government to accept the Bell Trade Act before any individual war damage claims in excess of $500 were to be paid. A heated debate took place in the Philippine Congress. Roxas pushed hard in favor of this bill; it passed by only one vote and was approved by the voters in the plebiscite in March 1947.

Thus, the U.S. government indirectly ensured its economic control and protected its business interests. In exchange for desperately needed reconstruction and rehabilitation aid to help to rebuild the country after the war, the Americans pressured the Filipinos into accepting the unfair Bell Trade Act. After accepting the rehabilitation aid, President Roxas had to concentrate on fighting the so-called Communist threat in the countryside, until he died of a heart attack on April 16, 1948, and was succeeded by his Vice President Elpidio Quirino.

QUIRINO ADMINISTRATION (1948–1953)

Elpidio Quirino, having succeeded President Manuel Roxas upon the latter's death in April 1948, became a candidate for the presidency at the election in November 1949. He was opposed by Jose Laurel, former president of the Japanese-sponsored republic and nominee of the Nationalist Party, which had attacked Roxas for collaboration in 1946. His other opponent was Senator Jose Avelino, former president of the Senate and leader of the Liberal Party, who was ousted from both posts on charges of selling war surpluses, and led a rebel wing, while Quirino headed the main Liberal Party. The election held on November 8 was scandalized by violence and fraud. The outcome of the election had essentially already been decided. The Liberal Party had more men and more money, and more than half the votes were for Quirino.[5] A short-lived rebellion broke out in Batangas, Laurel's home province, after the election. President Quirino's Liberal Party won a majority in Congress, controlling about 60 of the 100 seats in the Congress. Inauguration of the new officials took place in December 1949.

The way in which the elections were rigged by the Liberal Party had a significant impact on the way it ruled the nation, as corruption begets corruption. The elections took place in the middle of military campaign against the HUKs, who as discussed in the last chapter successfully fought against the Japanese forces during World War II. Composed largely of rural peasants and farmers, the HUKs were actually more inclined toward legal means of struggle and wanted land reform and greater social and economic justice. But, the earlier Roxas administration refused to allow them to enter the framework of the political process and declared them a seditious and illegal organization for their Communist leanings in March 1948. Although Quirino, initially took a more conciliatory stance toward the HUKs by opening up negotiations, the talks fell apart when the HUK leaders refused to disarm until reforms had been made. The resultant military punitive expeditions against them only increased popular resentment against the government.

In July 1950, soon after the Korean War, President Quirino invited U.S. President Truman to send an Economic Survey Mission headed by Congressman Daniel Bell to make an intensive study of Philippine problems. In October, they reported that problems were low incomes and extremely low productivity, especially in the rural areas. Besides suggesting numerous changes aimed at raising incomes and increasing the participation of laborers and farmers in the economy, they recommended the provision of $250 million in U.S. aid to help carry out the new policies.[6] This aid was contingent on the Philippine government's taking steps to carry out these reforms. The agreement came at a moment when the country was on the verge of economic collapse, so it helped to buoy the Quirino government.

At the same time the United States was urging rural reform through the Bell Commission, they sent CIA advisers, notably Colonel Edward Lansdale, with the United States–Republic of the Philippines Military Group (JUSMAG), to take control of the counterinsurgency campaign against the HUKs. The aim of this campaign was two-fold, to launch an agrarian reform program while simultaneously conducting psychological warfare. Lansdale was assigned as the personal adviser to the Philippine secretary of state, Ramon Magsaysay, with whom he quickly became friends. They even became roommates at the JUSMAG complex.[7] Magsaysay traced his paternal lineage to a Chinese merchant who married a Filipina and settled in Zambales, a coastal province northwest of Manila. His father was a wealthy merchant and landowner, and his mother claimed descent from a Spanish noble. Born in 1907, the second of four children, Magsaysay dropped out of college and worked as a mechanic for his cousin's bus company. In 1941, when Japan invaded the country, he left his wife and three children to join a U.S. guerilla unit. He lent out vehicles to the U.S. forces and was placed in charge of all transportation in the province. When the war was over, Magsaysay was rewarded for his integrity by the U.S. Army with the title of military provincial governor, which launched his career in politics.[8] He became a member of the Liberal Party and was elected to Congress. He was later appointed secretary of national defense by Quirino, at the urging of the U.S. Embassy and JUSMAG.[9]

Under the advisement of Colonel Edward Lansdale, Ramon Magsaysay introduced sweeping changes in the organizational structure of the armed forces of the Philippines (AFP), transforming it into a more effective counterinsurgency fighting force. He oversaw the organization of paramilitary groups, such as the civilian guards, who were ordered to conduct psychological warfare operations against the HUKs. HUK members and civilian populations believed to be supporters of the HUKs were massacred by civilian guards under the discrete command of military officers. For example, "Magsaysay ordered his soldiers to act as though they were HUKs, often committing crimes and stirring up trouble in the countryside."[10] Colonel Lansdale devised "psywar" gimmicks such as broadcasting "voices" coming from the graves of dead HUK soldiers and making them look like victims of vampires (known as *aswangs* in Philippine folklore) to instill panic and fear in the local population.[11] The HUKs were defeated in October 1950, when the AFP captured the top leadership of the Communist Party in Manila.

The second part of Magsaysay's program was to win back the "hearts and minds" of the people for the government and away from the HUKs. Colonel Lansdale was involved in the Economic Development Corps, which was largely a propaganda tool used to resettle surrendered HUKs in areas far away from Luzon. The program included the use of military surveillance operations and equipment to clear large tracts of land in Mindanao for their resettlement. It was a huge success, and although the land grants actually benefited less than 1,000 families,[12] the media propaganda lured large numbers of poor families who voluntarily migrated, without financial aid, to set up their homesteads in Mindanao. The program was so successful that by 1960, more than a million people had spontaneously and without government support migrated to earn their livelihoods from farming in Mindanao.[13] After these moves against the HUKs and economic incentive programs came the elections of 1951. A bill had been passed through Congress abolishing "block voting," and because local politicians and warlords were using their personal armies to garner votes, President Quirino supported Magsaysay's proposal to use the army and a private CIA-initiated organization, National Association for the Maintenance of Free Elections (NAMFREL), to guard the polls. This move made for a more peaceful and honest election than in 1946 and 1949. The Liberal Party lost to the Nationalistas all nine Senate seats and 23 of 52 provincial governorships.

The Nationalista Party leadership nominated Magsaysay for the presidential campaign of 1953, after which he resigned from the Liberal Party and cabinet post and began his campaign. He was backed by the professional military officers, the U.S. CIA, the Catholic Church, professional associations, and anti-Communist labor and peasant associations, which formed the Citizens for Good Governance campaign that created a media image of him as "an ordinary guy" who worked his way up. He went on speaking engagements throughout the countryside, promising land reform and an end to corruption. In contrast, President Quirino, who was undergoing surgery for stomach ulcers in the

United States, built his campaign mainly by attacking his opponent for being an American puppet. On the day of the elections, the U.S. military advisers were stationed around the country observing the Philippine troops protecting the polls, while U.S. warships sailed into Manila Bay.[14] Magsaysay was on the deck of one of these ships when the election results came in and won almost two-thirds of all the votes cast.

MAGSAYSAY ADMINISTRATION (1953–1957)

The presidency of Ramon Magsaysay was the first postwar appearance of Filipino populism. During his first term in office, he passed the Republic Act, which was intended to increase the power of the executive branch and improve management of the state budget. He initiated a five-year economic development plan to generate 1.7 million jobs. Magsaysay recruited business executives and technical experts to implement economic projects. He persuaded the landlord-dominated Congress to pass the Agricultural Tenancy Act (1954) and established the Agricultural Tenancy Commission and the Land Tenure-Administration to deal with tenancy problems as well as the Agricultural Credit and Cooperative Financing Administration. It was during his term that the Retail Trade Nationalization Act was passed (1955), and the first major attempt was made to revise the Military Bases Agreement to bring its provisions more in line with Philippine interests.

Magsaysay opened up channels of communication with the common people. He spent a lot of time traveling through the countryside to listen to the barrio people's complaints and tried to resolve them on the spot. He brought numerous citizens into contact with the government, many for the first time, and demonstrated that political change was possible within the government. Yet, his personalized approach and self-emphasis prevented the full implementation of what he was trying to change. No matter how effective government agencies may have been through their personal connections with Magsaysay, their ongoing value as individual institutions with decision-making power was hampered by their association with the president.[15] Magsaysay's use of the army, for example, overrode the power of the local police, who worked for the landlords and politicians who had congressional clout. Congressmen watered down Magsaysay's Land Reform Act (1955) by adding amendments that exempted the large sugar estates, which made it nearly impossible for tenants to acquire land. Magsaysay's style was that of a traditional politician during the pre-commonwealth era, using his popularity to make changes to strengthen the country, while also trying to boost his status as a leader.[16] However, he was the first postwar president to mobilize the masses as a social force.

On March 16, 1957, President Magsaysay died in an airplane crash in Cebu, and the nation, shocked by this tragic event, went into mourning. The next day, Vice President Carlos Garcia was inducted into office and became the next president of the Republic of the Philippines.

PRESIDENT CARLOS GARCIA (1957–1961)

The fourth president of the Republic of the Philippines, President Polestico Carlos Garcia, was a brilliant statesman who was at ease with traditional patron-client relationships. He was once described as "of amiable personality, with a high intellect and sonorous eloquence, he was a lover of democracy, a good chess player, friendly in his dealings with people, and never vindictive to his enemies."[17] He completed Magsaysay's term, after which he was nominated by the Nationalista Party to run for reelection; however, the Nationalista Party that nominated him primarily consisted of the pre-Magsaysay members. The newer members who earlier formed the Magsaysay for President Movement broke away to form the Progressive Party. Garcia's vice presidential candidate was House Speaker Jose Laurel Jr. Their opponents were Jose Yulo of the Liberal Party, with Congressman Diosdado Macapagal as running mate; Manuel Manahan of the Progressive Party, with Vicente Araneta as running mate; Senator Claro Recto of the Nationalista-Citizen Party, with Senator Lorenzo Tanada as running mate; and Antonio Quirino, former President Quirino's younger brother, running for president on the rebel liberal ticket.

In this unprecedented and multisided election process, Garcia won, but only by a minority vote of 41 percent. He failed to carry with him Jose Laurel Jr., and Macapagal of the Liberal Party was elected vice president. This was the first time that Filipinos elected a president and vice president belonging to opposing parties.

President Garcia is best remembered for his Filipino First policy. A proponent of nationalism and democracy, he wanted to take back the local economy for the benefit of Filipinos. He promoted industrialization and offered special incentives to Filipino investors. This policy was not well received by the American business community or the Chinese and Chinese Filipino business community, because the latter felt that its interpretation of what it meant to be a Filipino was discriminatory against them. Nevertheless, under Garcia's administration, the industrial sector flourished, and, by 1960, there were some 5,000 industries, and the Filipino share of investments in these industries grew to 88 percent.[18] The production of domestic consumer goods and secondary industries, like manufacturing of machine parts and cement production, created new jobs, which propelled the rapid expansion of urban centers, especially Manila and Cebu.

However, it is documented that Garcia's Filipino First policy still benefited the rich more than the common Tao as follows:[19] In 1957, the top 20 percent of Filipino families received 55 percent of the total income, while the lowest

20 percent received only 4.5 percent. There was still a middle class, but it was stagnant. There were no more revolutionary peasant movements, mainly because of the disappearance of the radical Left and the ameliorating influence of reformist peasant and urban workers' associations, and the availability of land in Mindanao. The government and the Catholic Church hierarchy also implemented a pervasive anti-Communist propaganda system in the schools and churches.

In other words, it was the Filipino business elites who profited from Garcia's Filipino First policy, especially those who were Nationalista supporters. As Garcia explained, when it came to corruption, his government had become "a ship that has gathered a lot of barnacles along the way; I cannot shake them off...This was during a time of controls when it was so easy to make anybody a millionaire; just give them a license and its done."[20] Warlord politicians who commandeered their own personal armies engaged in illicit and profiteering business practices through their connections to the Nationalista political machine. National enterprises such as the National Development Corporation became infested with corruption, bribery, fraud, and favoritism. While there was a good deal of professionalism and integrity among the ranks, it was badly tainted by corruption and inefficiency. By the end of Garcia's term, the Filipino masses became disillusioned. The American and Chinese and Chinese Filipino businesses offset by the Filipino First policy protested more vehemently. They were joined by the middle classes who were upset by the resurgence of corruption. The American businesses and interests viewed Garcia's Filipino First policy as veering in the direction of socialism, much as Sukarno's socialist economic policies in Indonesia. Senior officers in the armed forces of the Philippines for the first time in the history began to engineer a coup, and opponents in Congress began a movement for Garcia's impeachment.

Garcia ran for president in the November election of 1961 and was defeated by the Liberal Party opponent, Diosdado Macapagal, with Senator Emmanuel Pelaez of the Liberal Party.

PRESIDENT DIOSDADO MACAPAGAL (1961–1965)

On November 14, 1961, Diosdado Macapagal was elected president by a margin of more than 600,000 votes.[21] He carried his vice presidential candidate, Emmanuel Pelaez, together with almost all of the senatorial slate of the Liberal Party. President Macapagal was a brilliant scholar, knowledgeable lawyer, and eloquent statesman. In 1948, he served as second secretary to the Philippine Embassy in Washington, D.C., and was elected to a seat in the Philippine Senate the following year, where he served until 1956. During this time, he served as the Philippine representative to the United Nations General Assembly. President Macapagal, as already mentioned, joined the Liberal Party in 1957 and served as vice president under the Nationalista president Carlos Garcia. In the 1961 election, however, he ran against Garcia, attracting to his banner the Liberal and Progressive parties to spearhead a popular campaign against political corruption, and was elected by a wide margin.

On December 30, 1961, Macapagal was inaugurated as the fifth president of the Republic of the Philippines. In his inaugural address, he promised to bring in a new era of prosperity. While president, he worked to suppress graft, corruption, and fraud and to stimulate the Philippine economy by opening it up for foreign investment and putting the peso on the free currency exchange market. His strong advocacy on behalf of free enterprise was, not surprisingly, well received by the Chinese, Chinese Filipinos, and American business communities, who banded behind him. The middle classes supported President Macapagal because they had developed new consumer desires and felt cut off from the flow foreign goods, especially American goods, by Garcia's Filipino First policy. Filipino intellectuals as well, at that time, were looking to President Macapagal to solve the most pressing problem of corruption and to implement a more rational development trajectory.

President Macapagal instituted the Program Implementation Agency, which was charged with designing and implementing a new national development plan. This agency was intended to counteract the National Economic Council, which had grown overly corrupt under the rule of politicians during the Garcia period. He recruited professional technocrats, especially American-trained technocrats, who shared his vision of an open economy; these professionals were well received by international donor agencies, such as the World Bank and International Monetary Fund. The Program Implementation Agency was instrumental in opening up the economy, which increased the exportation of agricultural products and temporarily raised the value of the peso. However, the tariffs that accompanied these acts reversed the desired effect as the main beneficiaries remained the Filipino oligarchy or the wealthy family owned conglomerates that diversified into new exports and industries.[22] These political families played their cards in Congress by stonewalling President Macapagal's projects.

The congressmen often refused to pass President Macapagal's bills or so watered them down with amendments as to destroy their purpose. Of the 26 bills that President Macapagal sent to Congress, only three became law.[23] The Agricultural Land Reform Code was passed by Congress on August 8, 1963, only after they tacked on more than 200 amendments and exempted real-estate lands and a special tax to finance this reform. The Land Reform Code abolished share tenancy and installed the leasehold system in its place, which was a significant step in the direction of resolving the peasant problem. President Macapagal promised to go after tax evaders, in particular, the wealthy families who cost the treasury millions of dollars each year. However, his real and

perceived actions against these families only provoked them to use their connections to bring down his administration. From 1962 to 1963, they orches-
trated a campaign in the *Philippine Free Press,* regularly releasing articles aimed
at maligning his character (they called him a dictator) and exposing government corruption and the lavish lifestyle of rich government officials alongside
their country men and women stricken with poverty. In addition, the elite
oligarchies used their powerful patronage networks and links to the House
of Representatives and Senate to cripple President Macapagal's reforms. An
analogy can be drawn between President Macapagal's term and the quandary
of politics in the Philippines, and not only the Philippines. On the one hand,
personalities and individual men and women only have the power to act, produce policy, and effect change. On the other hand, individual men and women
are corruptible, and the overaccumulation of wealth in the hands of only a few
families can be dangerous.[24]

   In the election in November 1965, President Macapagal and his vice-
presidential candidate, Senator Gerardo Roxas, were defeated at the polls.
President of the Senate, Ferdinand Marcos, and his vice-presidential candidate, Senator Fernando Lopez, were elected president and vice president.

POSTWAR POLITICAL BEHAVIOR

   The incumbent president Ferdinand Marcos and vice president Fernando
Lopez ran for office on the Nationalista ticket, but both were former Liberal
Party members. Their political maneuver of shifting party affiliations to run
for office was not unusual behavior in the Philippines of this time period.
Manuel Roxas set the precedent when he switched from the Nationalistas to
run against Sergio Osmena on the Liberal ticket. Ramon Magsaysay switched
parties to run for president against Elpidio Quirino. Still, the Liberals, who
were the majority in Congress at the time, were disgruntled and not in favor
of the "turncoat," Marcos, because they lost their seats when he became president. Philippine politics seemed to become more competitively individualistic
and less nationalistic than during the prewar years. As we shall see in the
next chapter, President Marcos began his term from the position of a minority
president but eventually garnered the support of his earlier allies.

   Ferdinand Marcos managed to win against Diosdado Macapagal because of
his connections to leading Filipino elite families who could deliver the votes.
He relied on traditional Illocano allies who controlled large parts of northern
Luzon through their control of local resources and use of their private armies.
He formed a powerful alliance with the well-placed Lopez family, who made
a fortune from sugar, and extended their holdings into newspapers, television
stations, and power utilities. The Lopezes' had political connections in Congress, and they used these assemblies to fight against the former Macapagal's

policies. When President Macapagal promised to catch tax evaders, especially the "big fish," the Lopezes' retaliated by using their media connections to expose widespread corruption in government. Feeding off the public's longing for good and fair governance, Marcos rode on the pledge that "he would make this nation great again." Ironically, however, as we will see in chapter 6, the Marcos government was one of the most, if not the most, repressive and corrupt governments in Philippine history.

Philippine politics after World War II evolved from what was a predominantly one-party system during the commonwealth era to a two-party system. The Nationalista Party was challenged by the breakaway faction that emerged as the Liberal Party.[25] The Liberal Party brought in new elites, who were educated under the commonwealth, and led guerilla units, which gave them enormous control over local resources and through whom war reparations and moneys were channeled after the war. These new elites did not feel the same allegiance to the nation that many of the prewar nationalist politicians did. They, conversely, viewed holding office not as an opportunity to serve but as a means to achieve greater wealth for themselves and their political interest group.

Meanwhile, as we have already seen in this chapter, the gross repression by the landlord politicians of the peasants over the years provoked them into open rebellion in 1949. The most notorious revolt was that of the HUKs of central and northern Luzon. They were against the Bell Trade Act, especially its addition of the parity clause to the constitution, and the U.S. Military Base Agreement and were for greater social and economic justice and land reform. With the rise of the Cold War, however, the U.S. government initiated a massive anti-Communist campaign and sent military experts and CIA advisers to help to fight the HUKs. CIA operative Edward Lansdale and Ramon Magsaysay greatly expanded and reorganized the Philippine military forces, transforming them into anti-insurgency and paramilitary operations, which, consequently, defeated the HUKs. The Nationalistas and Liberals, meanwhile, were showing no overt inclination to articulate radical views of the peasants, as their own nationalist views were in abeyance and decline.

However, as we shall see in the next chapter, the HUK's cause to improve the social and economic circumstances of the poor was rejuvenated and given new impetus by the student movement at the beginning of the 1970s, which reorganized the Communist Party of the Philippines. These students were intellectual idealists, and many came from upper- and middle-class families. Their movement was similar to the civil rights and anti-Vietnam war protest movements in the United States, the antiapartheid movement in South Africa, Gandhi's independence movement in India, and anti-imperialist and socialist student movements such as those place in France and elsewhere in Europe. They were ideologically aligned with Mao Tse Tsung's revolution in China and Ho Chi Min's Independence Movement in Vietnam. Philippine college students were also appalled at the contradictions in Marcos's government and the prevailing ethos bent on profit. Many university students were from the rural areas and had seen first-hand poor tenant farmers being harassed or even killed by Philippine military and paramilitary men for being so-called HUK sympathizers. The radicalization of the students, who supported and helped organize the peasants and other poor laboring classes, occurred in reaction to the increasingly repressive tactics of the Marcos government. As we shall see in chapter 6, the movement spread to include other social sectors, including religious practitioners, teachers, and the professional classes, as more and more citizens turned against the Marcos regime.

NOTES

1. Jean Grossholtz, *Politics in the Philippines* (Boston: Little, Brown and Company, 1964), p. 36.

2. David Wurfel, "The Philippines," in *Governments and Politics of Southeast Asia,* ed. George McTurnan Kahin (Ithaca: Cornell University Press, 1964), p. 697.

3. This same tactic would be employed again and again by future Filipino politicians running for president; for example, in the next presidential election of 1949, Elpidio Quirino, Roxas's vice president and successor when he died in office, was nominated by the Liberal Party, while Jose Laurel of the same party lost the nomination. Instead of bowing out of the elections, Jose Laurel formed a new radical wing of the Liberal Party and ran for president against Quirino, while Jose Laurel was the presidential nominee of the Nationalista Party. In the subsequent election campaign of 1953, Quirino was the nominee of the Liberal Party, while Ramon Magsaysay lost the nomination. So, Magsaysay switched sides to obtain the nomination of the Nationalista Party. In the next presidential campaign of 1957, Magsaysay's vice president, Polestico Carlos Garcia, who succeeded him when he died in office, was the nominee of the Nationalista Party. But Garcia was the choice of the more traditional politicians who predated the arrival of Magsaysay. The newer cohort that had formed the Magsaysay for President Movement did not agree with their party's nomination decision, so they broke away to form a new Progressive Party, nominating Manuel Manahan. Another faction also split from the main Nationalista Party to form the Nationalista-Citizen Party, which nominated Senator Claro Recto. Meanwhile, the Liberal Party nominated Jose Yulo, but a younger faction did not agree and broke away to nominate Antonio Quirino, who ran for president on the rebel liberal party ticket.

4. Jean Grossholtz, *Politics in the Philippines*, p. 37.

5. David Wurfel, "The Philippines" in *Governments and Politics of Southeast Asia,* ed. George McTurnan Kahin, p. 700.

6. Ibid.

7. James Putzel, *A Captive Land, The Politics of Agrarian Reform in the Philippines* (Manila: Ateneo de Manila Press, 1992), p. 88.

8. Stanley Karnow, *In Our Image, America's Empire in the Philippines* (New York: Ballantine Books, 1989), p. 349.

9. Stanley Karnow, *In Our Image, America's Empire in the Philippines*, p. 347.

10. James Putzel, *A Captive Land, The Politics of Agrarian Reform in the Philippines*, p. 88.

11. Stanley Karnow, *In Our Image, America's Empire in the Philippines*, p. 351.

12. Ibid.

13. Patricio Abinales and Donna Amoroso, *State and Society in the Philippines* (Rowman & Littlefield Publishers, 2005), p. 175.

14. Stanley Karnow, *In Our Image, America's Empire in the Philippines*, p. 353.

15. Patricio Abinales and Donna Amoroso, *State and Society in the Philippines*, p. 181.

16. Ibid.

17. Sonia Zaide, *The Philipppines, A Unique Nation* (Quezon City: All Nations Publishing Co., 1999), p. 361.

18. Patricio Abinales and Donna Amoroso, *State and Society in the Philippines*, p. 182.

19. Patricio Abinales and Donna Amoroso, *State and Society in the Philippines*, p. 183.

20. *Philippine Free Press*, July 8, 1972, quoted in Lewis Gleeck Jr., *The Third Philippine Republic, 1946–1972* (Quezon City: New Day Publishers, 1993), p. 212; and Patricio Abinales and Donna Amoroso, *State and Society in the Philippines*, p. 183.

21. David Wurfel, "The Philippines" in *Governments and Politics of Southeast Asia*, ed. George McTurnan Kahin, p. 707.

22. Patricio Abinales and Donna Amoroso, *State and Society in the Philippines*, p. 185.

23. Ibid.

24. Jean Grossholtz, *Politics in the Philippines*, p. 174.

25. Patricio Abinales and Donna Amoroso, *State and Society in the Philippines*, p. 189.

6

The Marcos Regime
(1965–1986)

In 1965, when Ferdinand Marcos was elected president, the Philippines had been considered by its neighbors to be a showcase for democratic development. At that time, it had a newly burgeoning and strong middle class and one of the highest literacy rates in the region. It held regular elections and had a functioning Congress and highly effective and legitimate Supreme Court. Over the next 20 years, Marcos took apart this democracy and constructed an authoritarian government that lasted until he was ousted from office by a massive People Power revolution in February 1986. Significantly, Marcos resorted to borrowing from outside and inside donors to pay for infrastructure projects. In exchange for loans from the World Bank and International Monetary Fund, he further opened up the economy and removed existing trade restrictions on transnational corporations, which markedly increased the national debt. His government continued the process, begun by former President Macapagal, of hiring western-trained technocrats to plan development. Also, Marcos greatly increased the size of the military and expanded its role in governance. His economic, political, and militaristic restructuring program melded well with U.S. foreign policy at the time, which favored export-driven and top-down development and strengthening the military to fight against the so-called Communist threat.

THE BIOGRAPHY OF MARCOS

Ferdinand Marcos devised his public image to appear to be the embodiment of the Filipino soul, much in same way that ancient Asian emperors were deified as incarnations of their people's spirit. Like the sculpted heads of kings looking down from temple steeps at Angkor Wat, Marcos had his own bust carved into a hillside in central Luzon.[1] He depicted himself to be, at once, of noble, peasant, warrior, artist, colonial, and nationalist descent, as if he were the collective spirit writ large. His wife, Imelda, once attempted to commission the painting of a large mural covering the broad spectrum of Philippine history with all the faces bearing a resemblance to the Marcos family.[2] Their first son, Ferdinand Jr., more commonly known as "Bong Bong," who was being groomed as Marcos's successor, was made governor of Illocos. Imelda was handed the governorship of Manila, a seat in the cabinet, and many other appointments. Marcos held court with foreign dignitaries and emissaries of state while seated on a golden thrown perched high above them. He disempowered potential opponents and surrounded himself with only those perceived to be loyal relatives and friends, like his former chauffer and cousin, General Fabian Ver, who was quickly promoted to general and then chief of defense.

Ferdinand Edralin Marcos was born on September 11, 1917, in the town of Surrat in Illocos Norte, a rugged rural province in northwestern Luzon. He was part of the provincial Filipino/Chinese elite class. His mother was an elementary school teacher who helped her parents run the family store. It is said that her ancestral line stemmed back to the original Chinese settlers, who intermarried with local Filipinas under Spanish colonialism. They collaborated by helping to collect tribute and administrate governmental affairs. Marcos's father was a public school supervisor who later became a politician. His grandfather, Fructuoso Edralin, is reported to have owned about 200 acres (80 hectares) of prime irrigated rice fields and coffee plantations and an additional 120 acres (50 hectares) of land outside of Surrat. During the American colonial era, he purchased 250 acres (100 hectares) of pure virgin forest land and sold timber to Chinese mills linked with his wife's family, the Quetulios, a wealthy Chinese merchant-class family in Ilocos Sur.[3] Both Marcos's father and mother earned their teaching credentials under the Thomasites, who were American colonial missionaries who came to the Philippines to disseminate and propagate English-language acquisition, American values and history, and educational techniques. Mariano, Marcos's grandfather, was an illegitimate son of a rural Spanish judge. His grandfather on his father's side, Fabian Marcos, served as a mayor in the town of Batac.

There are many rumors surrounding Ferdinand Marcos's family background; some have been accounted for historically. Seagrave, in his 1988 biographical account *The Marcos Dynasty*, finds substantial evidence to suggest that Marcos's mother had an affair with Ferdinand Chua, the son of a leading wealthy Chinese family in Illocos. The Chua family opposed the marriage and instead arranged a marriage between Josefa Edralin and Mariano Marcos, whose political career took off as a result of his being backed by the powerful Chua family. Mariano and his family subsequently moved to Manila, where he graduated from the University of the Philippines in 1924. That same year, he was elected an assemblyman in the Congress. Josefa found a job as an elementary school teacher in Manila. There, the family networked and developed their alliances with politically influential urban and rural elites. Mariano served for two terms in Congress, the second under the Japanese occupation regime during World War II. He was later captured and denounced for collaboration and tied to four water buffalos by Filipino guerillas and pulled apart.[4] Ferdinand Marcos's "godfather," Ferdinand Chua, took an interest in and paid for his educational expenses and later helped to advance his political career. In 1930, Ferdinand Marcos enrolled at the University of the Philippines High School and, three years later, the University of the Philippines, Diliman Campus.

In 1938, at 21 years old, Ferdinand Marcos and his uncle, and later his father, were arrested for the assassination of Assemblyman Julio Nalundasan. Nalundasan had successfully defeated and "humiliated" Mariano in a race for congressional office in his home province in 1935. Shortly after the elections, he was murdered. Although one of Mariano's supporters was apprehended and accused, the case was thrown out of court for lack of evidence. After his arrest, Ferdinand Marcos received a great deal of press coverage and some notoriety because he successfully delivered his own plea for bail so that he could complete his law degree and prepare an appeal to the Supreme Court. Later, in 1939, Ferdinand Marcos was found guilty and sentenced to 17 years in jail. In prison, he wrote his appeal, took the bar exam, and earned the highest score in his class. The next year, Marcos successfully argued his case before the Supreme Court, which was presided over by Jose Laurel. According to Seagrave, however, it was Ferdinand Chua who worked behind the scenes and really managed to influence the Supreme Court to dismiss the solid testimony that had earlier convicted Marcos of murder. Marcos was freed and remained loyal to Laurel, to whom he owed *utang na loob* (a debt; literally, "gratitude from the heart").

During World War II, Ferdinand Marcos served as a lieutenant at Bataan and was awarded one medal of valor. He was captured and later released by the Japanese, after which there are no credible records of his wartime experiences. Could his father or President Laurel have interceded? It has been suggested that Marcos promoted his political career on the basis of assertions that he was a war hero and highly decorated veteran.[5] Marcos falsely claimed to have received 300 medals, including the U.S. Congressional Medal of Honor. He boasted of commanding a battalion, Ang Mga Maharlika, of 8,000 guerilla soldiers who fought against the Japanese in northern and central Luzon and sent intelligence information to the U.S. forces. One scholar noted that "Marcos's purported heroism was his rise to manhood, his profile in courage, his passport to political prominence, the symbol of his shared loyalty to America and the Philippines, his epiphany."[6] U.S. Army records found in the National Archives document that American officers rejected Marcos's plea for funds and supplies on the grounds that his movement was a fraud.[7] Although Marcos had some involvement with guerrilla units, it is possible that he was working for the Laurel administration during the Japanese occupation period.[8]

After World War II, Ferdinand Marcos was practicing law in Manila when President Roxus invited him, in 1946, to enter politics. Marcos joined the Liberal Party and in 1949, with the backing of his home province of Illocos, he successfully ran for a seat in the lower legislature. He served in the legislature for three years, and went on to win in the Senate election of 1959.

HIS PRESIDENCY

In the presidential elections in November 1965, Ferdinand Marcos changed his affiliation from the Liberal Party to the Nationalista Party to better position himself to run for office. President Macapagal and his running mate, Gerardo Roxas, of the Liberal Party were defeated at the polls, and the Nationalistas regained control of Congress. Senate President Marcos and Senator Fernando Lopez were elected president and vice president, respectively.

By the time Marcos was sworn into office in December 1965, the nation was facing serious economic challenges, as real economic power still rested in the hands of a few wealthy families. Marcos capitalized on the people's strong desire for good and fair government practices by campaigning under the banner that "This can be a greater nation." In his inaugural address, he stated: "The Filipino people, it seems, has lost his soul, his dignity, and his courage. Our people have come to a point of despair. We have ceased to value order. Government is gripping the iron hand of venality, its treasury is barren, its resources are wasted, its civil service is slothful and indifferent, its armed forces demoralized, and its councils sterile. Not one hero alone do I ask from you but many—nay, all."[9] Indeed, the national treasury was almost empty as corruption was endemic in the government of Macapagal. Although Macapagal tried to professionalize the state bureaucracy, his hands were tied by an unfriendly Congress, and his programs were never fully implemented. As the country was undergoing rapid modernization and urbanization, the cities were beginning to be overcrowded as rural-to-urban migrants moved in large numbers looking for waged work. But, opportunities for employment did not keep pace, and underemployment and unemployment were becoming major problems as the population kept growing. Also, student activists, labor unionists, and social and religious action workers began to critically question the imposition of the United States in the Philippines and Vietnam.

Marcos became president at a time when the economy had a highly trained and professional English-speaking workforce. The Philippines was being depicted abroad as the single most democratic nation-state in Asia. With the increasing buildup of the U.S. military forces against Communism, especially in Vietnam, and a few years earlier in Korea, the U.S. government highly valued its strategically located military bases in the Philippines, especially Subic Naval Base and Clark Air Base, which, at that time, were the largest U.S. bases in the world. President Lyndon B. Johnson wooed President Marcos by flattering him and showering him with praise for his adherence to "democratic" principles. The U.S. military bases in the Philippines served as an important staging ground for the war in Vietnam, while nearby Filipino communities were transformed into rest and recreation zones for the soldiers. This created a burst of economic activity in the Philippines. President Marcos, who knew how valuable these military bases were to the U.S. government, played his "base card" well. As a result, the United States began to pay rent for the use of these bases on Philippine soil.[10] American military assistance to the Philippines went up from $18.5 million in 1972 to $45.3 million the following year. The transfer of military equipment and training assistance also dramatically increased. A few years later, even U.S. President Jimmy Carter (1977–1981), who decried President Marcos for his notorious human rights record, gave him $500 million in security assistance.[11] Thus, President Marcos and his wife, Imelda, had access to an enormous amount of liquid cash, and they absconded with "the lion's share" of this money. While the prior government was certainly corrupt, Marcos and his wife were far more flagrant in their abuse of power. The Marcos government controlled and manipulated the television stations to create false media reports that he was initiating development projects.

Presidential elections were held again on November 11, 1969, when President Marcos and Vice President Lopez were elected for a second term. Their opponents were Senator Sergio Osmena Jr. and Senator Genaro Magsaysay of the Liberal Party. The Marcos campaign had a budget of US$50 million, by conservative estimates, and was one of the most fraudulent election campaigns in local history.[12] He spent a fortune on posters, billboards, and television advertisements. As seen in previous chapters, past elections had been rigged, but Marcos blatantly misused public funds to bribe political bosses into guaranteeing that they would bring in votes from their districts for him, at whatever cost, even through the use of their personal armies. Marcos employed his executive power to dominate and control Congress. Although Congress had the authority to designate how public money would be used, it was ultimately President Marcos, the highest official in the land, who had the power to say when the money could be released. Thus, he could stonewall

Congress. Marcos used his role to distribute government money like a reward to those who were loyal, while withholding funds from those he perceived to be disloyal. Ultimately, he was reelected president for a second term.

MARCOS DECLARES MARTIAL LAW

The Marcos government lost its legitimacy as formerly peaceful citizens began to engage in acts of civil disobedience. After the elections, a group of college student protesters marched on Malacanan Palace and were met by riot police who shot four dead at Mendiola Bridge. This bridge has since become a powerful national symbol in memory of their martyrdom and heroism. Demonstrators across the country were calling for good governance and an end to corruption; land reform for the tenants, farmers, and peasants; affordable housing, lower prices on prime commodities, and jobs for the jobless; improvements in the educational system; and a new constitution to replace the obsolete 1935 constitution.[13] They were concerned about the constitution because it gave too much power to the president. Also, it did not include provisions to prevent and redress election fraud.

In 1970, Marcos signed a congressional resolution that called for a convention to be held the following year to review the 1935 constitution. While this convention might have posed a threat to his stay in power, it was also an opportunity for Marcos to bribe delegates to change the 1935 prohibition against the president serving for more than two terms.[14] The next year, when the convention was being held, there was a countrywide election campaign going on for the selection of local government officials. Marcos staged several bombing incidents around the country, and, most notoriously, had his men throw a bomb into the center of a Liberal Party rally being held at Miranda Plaza in Manila.[15] Eight people were killed, and 120 others were injured. Among those wounded were Senator Gerardo Roxas and his wife, Senator Jovito Salonga (running for reelection), Senator Sergio Osmena Jr., Congressman John Osmena (senatorial candidate), Senator Eva Estrada Kalaw (guest candidate on the Liberal Party senatorial ticket), Congressman Ramon Mitra (senatorial candidate), Congressman Ramon Bagatsing (candidate for Mayor of Manila), and Laguna Governor Felicismo T. San Luis (master of ceremonies).[16] Senator Benigno Aquino had not yet arrived. Marcos leaked false information to the press that this incident was committed by the Communists, while, in fact, it was an engineered by Marcos to create the appearance of social unrest as an excuse to declare martial law. The Miranda Plaza massacre had the reverse effect of turning many more citizens against the Marcos government. The following year, in 1972, Marcos declared martial law and ruled the Philippines for a total of 20 years, until he was overthrown by a massive People's Power revolution in February 1986.

THE GREEN REVOLUTION

Shortly before Marcos declared martial law in 1972, central Luzon was targeted by his administration to be a development showcase for the Green Revolution. The Rockefeller and Ford foundations first initiated the Green Revolution in the Philippines in 1960, when they funded the establishment of the International Rice Research Institute in Manila, whose research still largely benefits transnational corporations. After Marcos declared martial law, the World Bank and the International Monetary Fund increased lending to the Philippines, up $165.1 million in 1974 from an average of $30 million per year in the previous five years.[17] Instead of emphasizing a more equitable distribution of land, income, and resources, the technocratic model of the Green Revolution stressed only increasing production of crops for sale in the market as a way to solve the poverty problem. The tenants of central Luzon received government incentives, new high-yield hybrid varieties of rice that produced more only if pesticides and fertilizers were used, drawn from this funding to increase farm production. However, the cost of the new rice technology was high as compared to traditional forms. In times of bad harvests, small farmers began to mortgage, and then lose, their land to repay their loans. The high-yielding rice varieties required costly chemical pesticides and petroleum-based fertilizers that depleted soil fertility and ecological diversity in agriculture. Although chemical inputs and artificial fertilizers may be good for plants, they are unhealthy for human consumption. While the Green Revolution benefited wealthy farmers, agribusiness, and large landowners, who grew richer from increasing production, it had a negative impact on small farmers and poor landless farmers.

Some questioned whether martial law was able to change the pattern of politics in central Luzon into class-based parties and organizations at the local level as it proposed to do. It was argued that in contrast to those who perceive the Philippines as a state structured along patron-client lines, such ties have changed into new types of relationships that do not fit traditional patterns. That is, there are patron-client relations between the president and upper-class politicians, and between those elites and local brokers who bring in the votes, but the relations between local elites and peasants have none of the security of traditional reciprocity. It can be explained that "these new relations between politicians and the electorate are short-term, instrumental, impersonal, and based on a specific transaction if any. They are completely different from the multifaceted, dyadic relations that linked landlords and tenants in the good old days."[18] The landlords tried only to outwit tenants, and to make a profit from them, while tenant farmers were still thinking in terms of a subsistence economy. In fact, patron-client relations do not form a unifying state structure in the Philippines. Rather, they are a structure tied into wider processes of state development.

From the mid-1960s to the mid-1980s, Marcos depended on the Green Revolution's technology to promote his development of export agriculture as a major source of income and foreign exchange. Shortly after he declared martial law, there was a boom in the gross national product (GNP), and the economy entered a period of some recovery. Marcos's reliance on borrowing from external sources to fund development resulted in increased activity in export agriculture. However, the GNP is only a measure of improvements being made at the level of infrastructure (new construction; increases in the levels of electricity being used; improvements in transportation; increasing numbers of tourists). Consequently, changes in the GNP are not a clear indication that the quality of life went up for the average citizens. To the contrary, it was Marcos and his network that benefited most from this burst in export agriculture. Marcos used martial law to expropriate sugar and coconut industries, tobacco and beer, and other private enterprises that were nationalized and appropriated by his government.[19] It has been documented that Marcos used martial law to acquire the La Carlota sugar central of Negros Occidental, 30,000 hectares in the province of Cagayan and Isabela, and several hundred hectares in Davao, other parts of Mindanao and Panay.[20] There are other similar examples.[21] Marcos was able to get the largest share of profits from traditional export crops of sugar and coconut. He extracted income from the agricultural elite as a whole; then, he redistributed that income to a smaller inside subset of that class. Meanwhile, pineapples and bananas were becoming more important to transnational agribusiness industries. Forestry exports brought in substantial foreign exchange earnings. The benefits in each case were highly concentrated in the hands of Marcos and his network, while the "external costs" of his export-oriented development program were imposed on the Filipino people.[22]

MARCOS'S FALL

Given the preponderantly religious population of the Philippines, it should come as no surprise that when Ferdinand Marcos declared martial law on September 21, 1972, which lasted until 1986, he met resistance. The Moro National Liberation Front, a separatist movement founded by Nur Misuari in 1968, enlarged its revolutionary war against the Marcos regime. Thousands of people, including civilians, died when Marcos declared martial law and dispatched his military operations in Mindanao, while hundreds of thousands sought refuge in Sabah and East Malaysia before a ceasefire could be arranged in 1976. The New People's Army, the military arm of the Communist Party of the Philippines, which was established in 1969, 27 years after the HUK army, was able to establish many more armed units and networks after Marcos declared martial law than before.[23] Christian social activists and affiliated nongovernmental organizations (NGOs) were relentless in their struggle for poor people's rights and, more broadly, human rights.[24] Even the conservative Roman Catholic hierarchy engaged in what it referred to as "critical collaboration." Critical collaboration made it possible for the Roman Catholic Church to retain its institutional authority and autonomy, while maintaining its international networks and continuing its social action work in poor communities to help to ameliorate poverty, and to defend the poor against injustices.[25]

The conditions of martial law under the Marcos regime created a situation where the churches became politically more significant. Most other major institutions—the Congress, the courts, political parties, labor organizations, newspapers, and public broadcasting networks—were severely repressed by the military under the Marcos dictatorship. As a result, the coalition of churches, especially but not exclusively the Catholic Church, emerged as a major voice for the rights of the poor and oppressed inside the nation. Filipino Catholicism, being the dominant religion, has a long history of social activism in the Philippines. The historical roots of the nationalist movement against the Marcos dictatorship can be traced back to the 1896 Philippine revolution against Spain. At that time, a nationalist movement led by Catholic priests, professionals, and students gained a strong following. As we have already seen in chapter 3, for example, an uprising in Cavite in 1872, compelled the Spanish to arrest three pacifist diocesan priests, Jose Burgos, Mariano Gomez, and Jacinto Zamora, who were garroted to death for inciting "subversion." During the 1898 fight for independence from Spain, numerous revolutionaries were captured and executed, including the pacifist literary scholar, Jose Rizal, who was killed by a firing squad. Hence, the 1986 popular movement that arose to over throw Ferdinand Marcos gained some strong impetus from this history.

More specifically, the contemporary revolution was triggered by the brutal assassination of Benigno S. ("Ninoy") Aquino Jr. on September 21, 1983, upon his return from a three-year exile in the United States to run against Marcos in the upcoming presidential election. As soon as he landed at Manila International Airport, he was arrested and shot by one of Marcos's soldiers, who had supposedly been sent to guard him. His assassination was seen around the world on live television, and he became a national hero and martyr.

Of the five Philippine presidents whom Ninoy Aquino knew, only Marcos disliked him. When Marcos was first elected president, Ninoy Aquino was elected to the Senate. He stood up to Marcos and exposed corruption in government and, in 1968, was voted one of the most outstanding senators in the country. After the elections of 1969, he began to prepare to run against Marcos in the next presidential election in 1973. But Ferdinand Marcos declared martial law, and 10 minutes after midnight on September 22, 1972, Ninoy Aquino was arrested at the Manila Hilton Hotel. He was the first of hundreds of those who criticized the government to be rounded up and detained. Gradually, many of the detainees were released, but Ninoy and another outspoken critic, Senator Jose Diokno, were not. During seven years of confinement, Ninoy was tortured and isolated; he challenged the farcical military courts by not accepting their verdicts. In March 1975, when his case was brought to trial again, Aquino went on a hunger strike that was widely covered in the international press and carefully watched by human rights groups: "Some people suggest I beg for mercy," said Aquino, "but I would rather die on my feet with honor, than live on bended knees with shame."[26] Aquino was transformed by the experience, through prayer, writing poetry, listening to music, and reading prolifically.[27]

In November 1977, a military tribunal declared Ninoy Aquino guilty, and he was given a death sentence. But, by 1978, Marcos held an election, and his opponents made Ninoy Aquino their rallying cry and symbol because they knew that the elections would be rigged. Ferdinand and Imelda Marcos were worried that if they had him executed, he would become a martyr, and yet they felt too threatened by his charisma to release him.[28] The next year, Ninoy Aquino suffered a heart attack, and the doctors recommended heart surgery in Texas. Cory Aquino had been working for years behind the scenes to try to secure exile for her husband, and finally, this was the opportunity for the Marcoses' to save face. Once in the United States, Aquino underwent surgery, and the family settled in Boston, Massachusetts, where Ninoy was given a political science fellowship at Harvard University.

In January 1981, Marcos suddenly lifted martial law and ran for reelection unopposed. By that time, he had lupus erythemotosus, a degenerative disease that attacked his kidneys. He was on dialysis, had kidney failure, and had undergone several transplants. There were rumors that Imelda and General Fabian Ver were waiting to proclaim themselves as the new president and vice president. Two years later, in 1983, Ninoy decided to try to pursue a alternative peaceful course for change by returning to the Philippines. Despite the warnings of Imelda and others that if he returned they could not guarantee his safety, he thought he could convince Marcos to hold another election. Imelda threatened Japan Airlines with loss of landing rights in Manila if it gave him passage.[29] Aquino flew a roundabout route reaching Taipei on August 20 and Manila on August 21, 1983. As he stepped off the plane, he was shot in the back of the head by one of the guards sent to escort him.

About two million people showed up at his funeral to pay tribute to the late senator. The funeral was the largest People Power movement in Philippine history, and it was not the last. The next year, in February 1984, Marcos called for a snap election, and Ninoy's widow, Cory, was lifted up by the people, who chanted "Cory, Cory, Cory for president." There was a debate within the traditional Left; the Communist Party decided to boycott the elections, which they assumed would be rigged. But, on February 7, 1986, Corazon Aquino was elected president of the Philippines, even as Marcos insisted that he had won. Cory was shown in the international media as holding the mandate of the people. There was a split in the military that had been building up gradually as a group of young officers organized the Reform the Armed Forces Movement (RAM). General Ver went after them, and they ran to General Ramos, who had graduated from West Point, and convinced him to join them. On February 22, Minister of Defense General Enrile and the vice chief of the armed forces seized two major bases in Manila, Camp Aguinaldo and Camp Crame. Enrile and Ramos, whose lives were in danger, approached the American Ambassador Stephen Bosworth; the archbishop of Manila, Jaime Cardinal Sin; and Cory Aquino. They endorsed Cory in exchange for protection. It was Archbishop Sin's call on the radio that brought thousands to surround Camp Crame and Camp Aguinaldo in support of this small military revolt against Marcos, which forced him into exile. Democracy had been restored, and Corazon Aquino assumed the presidency.

NOTES

1. Stanley Karnow, *In Our Image, America's Empire in the Philippines* (New York: Ballantine Books, 1989), pp. 366–377.

2. Interestingly, Imelda Marcos established the National Arts Center, which selectively housed artistically gifted children who were raised in this government school. After the fall of Marcos, one such prodigy, Eliseo Silva, migrated to Los Angeles. His large outside mural *Gintong Kasaysayan, Gintong Pamana* (A Glorious History, A Golden Legacy), which depicts the broad sweep of Philippine/Filipino American history, currently can be seen along Beverly Boulevard in Filipino Town, Los Angeles. For more details, interested readers are referred to Pearlie Rose S. Baluyut, "A Glorious History, A Golden Legacy: The Making of a Filipino American Identity and Community" in *Amerasia*, Vol. 24, No. 3 (Winter 1998), pp. 192–216.

3. David Joel Steinberg, *The Philippines, A Singular and Plural Place* (San Francisco: Westview Press, 1990), p. 111.

4. Sterling Seagrave, *Marcos Dynasty* (New York: Random House Publishing, 1988).

5. David Joel Steinberg, *The Philippines, A Singular and Plural Place*, p. 132.

6. Stanley Karnow, *In Our Image, America's Empire in the Philippines*, p. 369.

7. Alfred McCoy, "The Fake War Hero," *The National Times* (Sydney, Australia, January 24, 1986); "The Myth of the Maharlika," *Veritas* (Manila, Philippines, January 26, 1986).

8. David Joel Steinberg, *The Philippines, A Singular and Plural Place*, p. 133.

9. Patricio Abinales and Donna Amoroso, *State and Society in the Philippines* (Rowman & Littlefield Publishers, 2005), p. 115.

10. As part of the 1946 Bell Trade Act, the Philippine government was pressured into signing the Philippine–American Bases Agreement that allowed the U.S. to maintain its bases in the country for 99 years. This agreement has since expired. It came up for review and consideration for reinstatement in 1992 and was rejected by the Philippine Senate.

11. Patricio Abinales and Donna Amoroso, *State and Society in the Philippines*, pp. 210–211.

12. Resil Mojores, *They Man Who Would Be President: Sergio Osmena and Philippine Politics* (Cebu: Maria Cacao Publishers, 1986), p. 142; Stanley Karnow, *In Our Image, America's Empire in the Philippines*, p. 379; and, Patricio Abinales and Donna Amoroso, *State and Society in the Philippines*, p. 198.

13. Sonia Zaide, *The Philippines, A Unique Nation* (Quezon City: All Nations Publishing Co., 1999), p. 365.

14. David Joel Steinberg, *The Philippines, A Singular and Plural Place*, p. 116.

15. Patricio Abinales and Donna Amoroso, *State and Society in the Philippines*, p. 202.

16. Sonia Zaide, *The Philippines, A Unique Nation*, p. 368.

17. Walden Bello, David Kinley, and Elaine Elinson, *Development Debacle: The World Bank in the Philippines* (San Francisco: Institute for Food and Development Policy/Philippine Solidarity Network, 1982), p. 24.

18. Willem Wolters, *Politics, Patronage, and Class Conflict in Central Luzon*, (The Hague, Netherlands: Institute of Social Studies, 1983), p. 228.

19. Patricio Abinales and Donna Amoroso, *State and Society in the Philippines*, p. 213.

20. Benedict Kerkvliet, *The Huk Rebellion: A Study of Peasant Revolt in the Philippines* (Berkeley: University of California Press), p. 121.

21. See, especially, Belinda Aquino, *The Politics of Plunder: The Philippines Under Marcos* (Quezon City: Great Books Trading, 1987).

22. James Boyce, *The Philippines, The Political Economy of Growth and Impoverishment* (University of Hawaii Press, 1993), p. 10.

23. Patricio Abinales and Donna Amoroso, *State and Society in the Philippines*, pp. 207, 216–221.

24. Kathleen Nadeau, *Liberation Theology in the Philippines: Faith in a Revolution* (Westport, CT: Praeger Publishers, 2002).

25. Robert Youngblood, *Marcos against the Church, Economic Development and Political Repression in the Philippines* (Ithaca: Cornell University Press, 1990).

26. Ibid., p. 23

27. David Joel Steinberg, *The Philippines, A Singular and Plural Place*, p. 135.

28. David Joel Steinberg, *The Philippines, A Singular and Plural Place*, p. 136.

29. David Joel Steinberg, *The Philippines, A Singular and Plural Place*, p. 138.

7

The Philippines after Marcos

The assassination of Benigno ("Ninoy") Aquino in 1983 immediately made him a hero and martyr for the cause of national liberation. By then, most Filipinos had already experienced having a member of their own family, or someone they knew, harassed or, worse, exiled, forced into hiding, detained, tortured, or salvaged by the Marcos government. *Salvaged* is the colloquial term for abducted, murdered, and disappeared. Marcos and his wife, Imelda, were so flagrant in their abuse of power that Marcos had his military guards murder Ninoy Aquino in full view of the international press. Ninoy's mother left untouched the blood that covered her son's face to allow mourners to see the brutality of his murder, and the nation went into mourning. A million people flowed into the streets of Manila for his funeral procession. Cardinal Jamie Sin denounced Marcos in his closing address, and encouraged his flock to continue to persevere in their nonviolent movement to force him to step down.

On November 3, 1985, Marcos announced live on David Brinkley's morning show that he was going to hold a "snap election," a spontaneous election that was essentially a last-ditch attempt to regain the appearance of having been democratically elected into office. The moderate opposition agreed to participate in the electoral process and threw their support behind Corazon Aquino and Salvador Laurel for president and vice president, respectively. However, the harder line Communist Party boycotted the elections because they already knew that they would be rigged. In contrast, the president of the United States, Ronald Reagan, continued his support of the Marcos administration up until the very last minute. Ronald Reagan and his wife, Nancy, were first wooed by the Marcos couple back in 1969, when as governor of California, Reagan was sent to the Philippines to represent President Richard Nixon.[1] They were lavishly wined and dined by the first couple at a royal fiesta that outdid even the most luxurious of Hollywood bashes. The Marcos' gave a 10-million-dollar cash donation to the Ronald Reagan presidential campaign of 1984.[2] So, in return, when President Marcos declared himself the winner of the elections of 1985, President Reagan sent Vice President George Bush Sr., former director of the Central Intelligence Agency, to congratulate him. Ironically, in a toast for President Reagan, George Bush said, "We love your adherence to democratic principle—and the democratic process."[3] Even after Marcos had been overthrown, Reagan came to his rescue by providing the Marcos family with safe harbor in Hawaii. It is important to remember that Reagan actually was fully assessed of Marcos's atrocious human rights record and tyrannically corrupt form of government. As early as June 1984, the U.S. Embassy in Manila had sent a report written by James Nash to President Reagan explaining that insurgency was rapidly growing in the Philippines as a direct consequence of the Marcos regime's corruption, crony capitalism, and human rights violations. Admiral William Crowe, commander in chief of U.S. forces in the Pacific and top contender for the Joint Chiefs of Staff, backed Nash's report and added an addendum that the Philippine military was corrupt and demoralized under Marcos's cronyism; it needed to be professionalized because it had become incapable of fighting the insurgency. Still, Admiral Crowe was unable to convince Defense Secretary Casper Weinberger, CIA Director William Casey, and others from Reagan's inner circle to defect from Marcos's camp.[4]

Predictably, Marcos rigged the elections in November 1985, despite volunteers from the Nationalist Movement for Free Elections (NAMFREL) chaining themselves to the ballot boxes as they were being transported to the central counting sites. At the same time, there were numerous international observers and TV reporters who filmed corruption "live," as when the NAMFREL volunteers manning the computers in the central counting headquarters walked out in protest over the discrepancy between figures on an overhead screen that didn't match the figures on their computers. Meanwhile, there was defection within the middle ranks of the military as the young officers[5] for Reform the Armed Forces Movement (RAM) planned a coup against Marcos; however, General Ver found out and went after them. Together with their leaders, General Enrile and General Ramos, they secured themselves within Camp Crame and Camp Aguinaldo, and appealed to others in the military to support them. And, as discussed in the previous chapter, the two generals went for assistance to Cardinal Sin, who sent hundreds of thousands of people to surround and protect the soldiers through the nonviolent revolution that was successful in deposing Marcos. A new era seemed to commence with Aquino's ascension into the presidency. Also, her People's Power revolution was followed by other pro-democracy movements, in Seoul Korea in 1987, in Tiananmen Square in 1989, in Rangoon in 1989, the fall of the Soviet Union in 1991, and the fall of the Suharto regime in Indonesia in 1998, among other examples.

This chapter looks at how the various forces maneuvered and imposed themselves on those who came to power during the post-Marcos era. They had to face the Philippines' most pressing problems. The biggest problems were poverty and the collapse of the economy, since Marcos had left the country in shambles. There was also the issue of political strife between the Left and Right and the Muslim separatists in Mindanao. Corruption at the highest levels, gambling and syndication in the police and armed forces, the terrorist organization of Abu Sayyaf, and the restoration of a democratic system of governance had to be addressed if reform was to be successful.

THE AQUINO PRESIDENCY (1986–1992)

Corazon Aquino was born the daughter of a wealthy family. Her father was Jose Cojuangco of Tarlac, and her mother was Demetria Sumulong, daughter of distinguished Juan Sumulong of Antipolo. She received a convent education in the Philippines and went to the United States, where she obtained a bachelor of arts degree in French and mathematics from the Catholic College of St. Vincent, run by Sisters of Charity in New York. After graduation, she returned to her homeland, where she met and married Benigno (Ninoy) Aquino Jr. on October 11, 1954. She led the quiet life of a Catholic housewife and mother of five children, until her husband was assassinated and she became the new leader of the People Power revolution. Corazon Aquino was democratically elected as the new president of the republic on February 25, 1986. She entered office on a pledge to fight corruption and poverty. She immediately established a revolutionary government under the Freedom Constitution, which was eventually replaced by the Constitution of 1987, drafted by the Constitutional Commission and ratified on February 7, 1987. This served as the basis for the restoration of democracy.

On May 25, 1986, in an effort to hasten the reconstruction of a democratic government, President Aquino established the Constitutional Commission. She appointed to this commission former senators, congressmen, judges of the Supreme Court, and conservative members of the Catholic hierarchy. There were 48 delegates selected, most of whom were upper-class, educated lawyers, not unlike the delegates almost a century earlier.[6] However, these appointments demonstrated President Aquino's goal of reestablishing the old order that existed prior to martial law.[7] For example, by not including members of peasant organizations on this commission, she missed an opportunity to formulate genuine land reform policies that could have reduced rural poverty and unrest.

Basically, the new constitution established a presidential form of government and reinstated many of the features of the 1935 constitution, including a bicameral legislature and an independent Supreme Court. The president is limited to one six-year term; senators to two six-year terms; presidents, vice presidents, and senators are elected by popular vote in national elections. Voters may vote for presidents and vice presidents from different or opposing parties. Representatives are elected by legislative districts, with an additional unspecified number to the registered party-list representing the different national, regional, and sector-based organizations that represent labor, peasants, the urban poor, indigenous cultural communities, women, and other underrepresented groups.[8] The constitution provided for the protection of private property, a centralized form of government, civil and political rights, the importance of education, and a bill of rights. It also included a provision for land reform. However, some found this land reform provision to be deceptive because it "allows for land reform opponents to define the scope of land reform" as indicated in the following:

> The State shall, by law undertake an agrarian reform program founded on the right of the farmers and regular farm workers, who are landless, to own directly or collectively the lands they till or, in the case of other farm workers, to receive a just share of the fruits thereof. To this end, the State shall encourage and undertake the just distribution of all agricultural lands, subject to such priorities and reasonable retention limits as the Congress may prescribe, taking into account ecological, developmental or equity considerations, and subject to the payment of just compensation. In determining retention limits, the State shall respect the right of small landowners. The State shall further provide incentives for voluntary land sharing.[9]

The provision, while respecting the right of "small landowners," does not define the term *small landowner.* Implicitly, the provision states that the term refers to "teachers, clerks, nurses, and other hard working frugal people," but, at the same time, it lumps these small owners who cultivated their own land in the same category as "absentee landlords," whose land was farmed by tenants and farm workers. Also, this provision could actually limit the amount of land available for agrarian reform, and it provides constitutional mechanisms that could be manipulated by those landowners who seek to evade land redistribution.

Upon entering office, President Aquino's two most pressing challenges were how to deal with the economic crisis and the restoration of a democratic government. Marcos left the economy in shambles, causing a severe recession and the flight of capital from the Philippines. Poverty dramatically increased under his administration: social indicators show underemployment affected more than 20 percent of the labor force; real wages for skilled and unskilled labor declined from 100.0 in 1972 to 53.4 in 1980.[10] The Asian Development Bank provided data that ranked the Philippines below India, Indonesia, and Bangladesh in average per capita consumption, and the Ministry of Health documented that some four-fifths of Filipino children suffered from some form of malnutrition.[11] By the fall of Marcos's government, 50 percent of the total population was living in abject poverty.[12]

As a bailout effort, the International Monetary Fund (IMF) and World Bank restructured the national debt repayments, while exerting a formative influence over the political economy. Later, in 1989, the Aquino government was given a US$1.3 billion loan from the IMF on the condition that the liberalization of the economy (e.g., price decontrol, labor control, export-oriented development) continue, along with privatization of government-owned industries and institutions. Meanwhile, the responsibility for the provisioning of needed healthcare and social welfare was being increasingly shifted from the government to nongovernmental organizations (NGOs) and the churches. Gerard Clarke defines NGOs as "private, non-profit, professional organizations with a distinctive legal character, concerned with public welfare goals. Within this definition, NGOs include philanthropic foundations, church development agencies, academic think tanks, human rights organizations and other organizations focused on issues such as gender, health, agricultural development, social welfare, the environment, and indigenous people,"[13] and this definition is used here. Under Marcos, there was a proliferation of NGOs that arose to provide social services, since these services were not being adequately provided for by the government. Outside nonprofit donor organizations and churches directly funded nongovernment organizers to implement programs to help poor people succeed in improving their circumstances for themselves, by promoting income-generating projects and, in the agricultural sector, sustainable organic farming techniques, among other projects.

Politically, President Aquino became caught between three opposing forces: the Left and Right, and the traditional ruling elites from which her own family derived and that pressured her to protect their interests. Had she decided to promote social and economic programs for reform, the people's movement and their network of NGOs that had proliferated in reaction to the Marcos dictatorship would have supported her. Marcos already had replaced the traditional Nationalistas and Liberal parties with his own KBL Party (Kilusang Bagong Lipunan), which crumbled after his fall. So, there was no traditional political party when he was ousted; instead, there were numerous people's organizations and NGOs that came from different sectors but were united in their cause for greater equity and social and environmental justice. However, Aquino felt obliged to appoint members to her cabinet who were politically opposed if not outright antagonistic toward each other: From the conservative camp, she appointed General Ponce Juan Enrile, secretary of defense, and General Ramos, chief of staff. Her vice president, Laurel, represented the interests of the traditional ruling oligarchies. Then, from among her husband's moderate left-wing friends and associates who formed her campaign, she appointed Jaime Ong finance minister; Jose Concepcion, a businessman and co-founder of NAMFREL, minister of trade; Aquilino Pimentel minister of local governments; and Senator Jose Diokno, a world-class human rights lawyer, the head of the Presidential Commission on Human Rights. Solita Monsod became minister of economic planning. Joker Arroyo, her late husband's attorney and longtime human rights activist, was appointed executive secretary.[14]

She entered office when the nation's mood for major reform had reached its pinnacle, right after the fall of the Marcos regime. There were frequent and ongoing demonstrations in the streets, and the media, freed from the strictures of censorship, publicized a whole range of alternative political views, internal criticisms, and new possibilities for social change. But, Aquino did not have sufficient experience to govern and had to work with a military that she distrusted, for good reason.[15] The armed forces that she inherited was a creation of the Marcos dictatorship, and no sooner had she assumed power than did RAM (Reform the Armed Forces Movement) attempt to overthrow her government in May 1986. They made another attempt in November, in the first of a series of seven coups, which she quelled through the help of General Ramos. Fearing a military takeover, she appeared to have shifted her political allegiance to the right wing and made concessions. Those involved in the initial coup attempts were not punished. After the second coup, she asked for and accepted the resignations of four her own cabinet members who were longtime human rights advocates, including Secretary of Labor Bobby Sanchez, because they were being labeled Communist sympathizers by the military. With each subsequent coup attempt, she made more concessions, reneging on her promises of social change.

To her credit, Corazon Aquino is remembered for transitioning the Philippines from an authoritarian to a democratic form of government. Instrumental in this transition were reformist NGOs and people's organizations, which, even as Aquino moved to the right, continued to advocate for reform from below. Henceforth, in the Philippines, political and economic policies could not be so easily imposed from the top down, without taking into consideration the deliberations and responses of peoples' organizations and NGOs. Also, the Aquino administration passed the Republic Act 7160, Local Government Code of 1991 in an effort to decentralize some of the big powers of government. Under this legislation, local and provincial governments were given a larger share of the tax revenue and power to fund local development projects directly. Under subsequent administrations, NGOs and people's organizations continued to participate in this development arena at the local levels. During her six-year term, Aquino quelled seven attempts to overthrow her government, thereby preventing the return of a military dictatorship and effecting a peaceful and democratic transfer of power on June 30, 1992, when Fidel V. Ramos, the newly elected president, took office.

THE PRESIDENCY OF FIDEL RAMOS (1992–1997)

Fidel Valdez Ramos was born on March 18, 1928, in Lingayen, Pangasinan, Luzon. His father, Narciso Ramos (1900–1986), a lawyer and journalist, served as a legislator in the House of Representatives and was then appointed by former President Marcos as secretary of foreign affairs. His mother, Angela Valdez-Ramos (1905–1977), was a teacher and daughter of the influential Valdez family of Batac, Illocos Norte, which made Fidel Ramos a second cousin to Ferdinand Marcos. Fidel completed his elementary education in Lingayen, a high school in Manila, and earned a bachelor's degree in the United States, where he graduated from the West Point Military Academy in 1950. The following year, he earned his master's degree in Engineering from the University of Illinois. Fidel then became a career officer in the Philippine army, where he rose through the ranks. He served as 2ndlieutenant and infantry platoon leader in the Philippine Expeditionary Force in 1952, during the Korean War, and as chief of staff of the Philippine Civil Action Group in Vietnam from 1966 to 1968. He also helped organize the Philippine Special Forces, elite paratroopers trained to fight against insurgencies. In 1972, Marcos appointed him chief of the constabulary, the nationwide police force, and he served as one of Marcos's trusted advisers for twenty years. Fidel Ramos was responsible for enforcing martial law, when the constabulary arrested thousands of citizens for having criticized the Marcos government.

After the People's Power revolution erupted in February 1986, Fidel Ramos and Juan Ponce Enrile, the secretary of defense, switched sides and joined the presidential campaign of Corazon Aquino. Aquino assumed the presidency after the fall of Marcos. Under her administration, Ramos served as military chief of staff (1986–1988) and secretary of national defense (1988–1991), and he gained popular notoriety for preventing coups attempt against her government. At the end of Aquino's term, she endorsed and nominated him for the 1992 presidential election.

There was wide participation in the elections of 1992, which can be described as some of the most contentious elections in Philippine history.[16] Some 80,000 candidates ran for the 17,000 positions from the presidency on down to the municipal councilors. Fidel Ramos ended up loosing the nomination of the dominant party, Laban ng Demokratikong Pilipino (LDP), to House Speaker Ramon Mitra. Refusing to give way, he left the LDP to found his own new party, Partido Lakas ng Tao (People Power Party). Ramos invited Governor Emilio Osmena from Cebu to run as his vice president. His People Power Party formed an alliance with the National Union of Christian Democrats of Congressman Jose de Venecia and the United Muslim Democrats of Simeon Datumanong. It was also supported by many Filipino and Chinese Filipino business and traditional elite interests.

On May 11, 1992, Ramos won the presidential election but only by 23.58 percent of the vote, narrowly defeating populist Agrarian Reform Secretary Miriam Defensor Santiago. His vice presidential candidate, Osmena, lost to Joseph Estrada, who like former U.S. President Ronald Reagan, was a former senator and B-rated movie star. Ramos also appointed Vice President Estrada as chief of his Anti-Crime Commission. Significantly, six years later, Estrada won the presidential elections, but no sooner was he in office than he was ousted from power by a People Power II revolution. He was caught misusing the public trust (e.g., pocketing the national lottery earnings that had been previously earmarked for charities, accepting bribes and taking payoffs, etc.) and engaging in other illicit gambling and mafia activities, which had infected many police and government networks.

President Ramos began his term with a strong vision for making the Philippines a new economic "tiger" in Asia by the year 2000. In his 1993 State of the Nation address, Ramos proposed the following:

> A strategic framework for development which will be guided by a strong State. By a Strong State I mean one that can assert our country's strategic interests because it has relative autonomy over the influence of oligarchic groups. For the last 47 years, we have had a political system that has been too responsive to groups possessing wealth and power enough to bend the State to do their will. Such a political system has distorted our economy and rendered government ineffectual. This is the reason why the Philippines has lagged so far behind the East Asian Tigers.[17]

His "Philippine 2000," otherwise known as Medium Term Development Plan, promised to increase export-oriented industrialization and to further liberalize the economy to make it more attractive to outside investors. President Ramos increased the privatization and dismantling of existing state-owned monopolies, such as the domestic air carrier, shipping, telecommunications, and the oil industry.[18] And foreign investors gained renewed confidence in the republic, which appeared to have become politically stabilized. International and transnational investments in the "export processing zones" and other industrial complexes, for example, generated thousands of new jobs, which helped to re-invigorate the national economy, especially in Manila, central and northern Luzon, and Cebu.

However, President Ramos's "Philippine 2000" plan was not as well received inside the nation by the progressive and reformist NGOs and people's organizations that perceived it to be too focused on industrialization at the expense of agriculture. They had an alternative bottom-up development plan that focused on developing sustainable agriculture, such as organic farming, and building up industries that were directed above all to meet the practical needs of citizens. President Ramos's outward looking plan was contentious and met with serious resistance from social activists, human rights advocates, and nongovernment organizers working to improve poor people's lives. It was based on the illusionary model of catching-up development, as one labor rights advocate explained:

> Not all that glitters is gold. The silhouette of high-rise buildings with golden inscriptions on the façade does not always equate development. In the euphoria of boasting Cebu's economic opulence, much has been said about enticing foreign investors and tourists. Little is told about its dwindling agriculture, abject poverty, and about the consequences of what it means for the provincial economy to be perpetually a dependent satellite to foreign markets.[19]

In the anthropological literature, the illusion of catching-up development is based on the false belief that the only appropriate model of an affluent society is that prevailing in the United States, Western Europe, Hong Kong, Taiwan, Japan, and the Republic of South Korea. It implies that poor countries that follow the same path to industrialization and capital accumulation taken by modern industrial societies can achieve the same level of development. Yet, most of the richest nations of the world still have not attained a satisfactory level of development. In the United States, for example, real incomes and quality of life for many citizens have gone down steadily, especially in the post-9/11 period. Poor neighborhoods in Los Angeles and New York City, for example, are often dangerous places overtaken by drugs, gangs, and violence. Also, there are many citizens living in deprived circumstances in some of the most highly developed countries of the world, while the material conditions for most citizens in poor countries are getting increasingly worse.

The illusion of catching-up development is based on an evolutionary, linear understanding of history. The concept in Western Europe and North America has been mistakenly used by anthropologists such as James Steward and Leslie White to categorize societies and cultures according to their level of technological development. Economic specialists made theories of development consisting of the transfer or technology from richer to poorer countries. However, their projections, based on neoclassical economic theories that are functionalist and not universally applicable, failed. Prior to the breakup of socialism in Eastern Europe, orthodox Marxists also used the concept of catching-up development to depict world history as a series of stages (primitive, Communist, ancient, Asiatic, feudal, capitalist, Socialist, and advanced Communist). Each particular historical epoch was portrayed as being dominated by a particular mode of production and evolved into a new type through revolution. But nondogmatic and creative Marxists such as Maurice Godelier[20] have argued that Marx never intended his theory to be transformed into a suprahistorical theory to be imposed on other people. Mechanistic interpretations of evolutionary development have been criticized by nondogmatic Marxists and postmodernists of a neo-Marxist persuasion for ignoring different cultural proclivities. They have argued that the poverty of underdeveloped countries is not a result of some lag but the direct consequence of the overdevelopment of rich industrial countries that exploit the poor in Africa, Latin America, Asia, Eastern Europe, Russia, and elsewhere, as in war-torn Iraq and Afghanistan.

Up until the 1980s, international organizations such as the World Bank and IMF poured money into the Philippines to build up the infrastructure to speed the flow of goods for export. This resulted in a huge inflow of capital, as the Philippines became incredibly more indebted. By the time of the Aquino administration in 1986, the emphasis of international organizations had switched to restructuring the Philippine debt and funding smaller-scale development projects through the NGO sector.

Subsequently, the government continued to find itself in the precarious position of not being able to provide a living wage for the majority of its citizens, whose taxes, in turn, cannot prop up the state, although remittances sent back home by overseas Filipino workers have helped to fund the state's external debt repayments. Thus, the nonprofit sector of NGOs and people's organizations are expected to provide for human services that under ordinary circumstances would be the responsibility of the government. This creates an untenable situation. On the one side, international lending organizations prefer local NGOs because they are cost efficient and rely primarily on volunteer labor and financial support from churches and human rights organizations in the richer countries. On the other side, the NGOs and people's organizations are calling for land reform and sustainable use of natural resources to meet local needs. Paradoxically, President Ramos's "Philippine 2000" plan was created in light of complex global economic forces that maneuver to create circumstances (e.g., removing trade restrictions, decontrolling the peso, opening up previously restricted sectors to foreign ownership, and keeping wages low) attractive to outside investors to make export-oriented development possible.

By the time he left office, Ramos had won back the confidence of transnational and international investors in the Philippines, which generated some US$20 billion worth of outside investments.[21] Significantly, he went after state monopolies like the Cojuangco-owned Philippine Telephone Company, which controlled nearly all national and international long-distance services coming out of the country. By 1996, there were 13 different companies, most co-owned with foreigners, competing to provide landed and wireless services at substantially lower rates.[22] In 1998, Ramos ended the nation's economic dependency on the IMF, which largely was a result of the sale of Fort Bonifacio to private developers in 1996.[23] Remarkably, this feat was achieved at a time when many Asian neighbors were seeking more IMF loans.

In 1997, the Asian economic crisis swept through the region and negatively impacted the Philippines. The peso's worth had diminished, and this left banks and other corporations essentially bankrupt.[24] The Ramos government tried to strengthen the peso and lessen capital flight by selling as much a $4.5 billion, but this ended up depleting foreign reserves before allowing the peso to float. Domestic industries overly dependent on imports were hard pressed, causing increased unemployment. Still, the Philippines came out of the crisis positioned for economic recovery. It had fared better than many of its neighbors and managed to avoid experiencing a nationwide banking crisis, as had happened in nearby Thailand and Indonesia.

President Ramos ended his six-year term with a move for a "Cha Cha," or Charter Change, to amend the constitution by calling a constitutional convention, which failed to garner needed support. The "Cha Cha" was his attempt to run for reelection, which alienated many of his earlier supporters, especially government-and church-based allies. Many NGOs and people's organizations were already against his economic policies. President Ramos's administration had failed to satisfactorily address the pressing problem of crime as syndicated criminal activities increased. Human rights abuses committed by his military police and paramilitary forces against nonviolent labor activists, church workers, journalists, nongovernment organizers, and supporters in the urban and rural poor communities continued unabated. Those arrested were framed for common crimes that they did not commit, which made it hard for outside rights organizations such as Amnesty International to petition on behalf of individual political detainees since they were officially listed as common criminals.[25] While President Ramos is remembered for better positioning the Philippine economy in the global scheme, his attempt at prolonging his term in office, coupled with the increasing crime and rise of syndicated activities and kidnappings, caused many citizens to loose confidence in his government.

In the elections of 1998, President Fidel Ramos and the government party Lakas endorsed the presidential candidacy of Senator Jose de Venecia and vice presidential candidacy of Gloria Macapagal Arroyo, the daughter of former president Diosdado Macapagal. There were a number of opposing presidential candidates, including outgoing vice president, Joseph Estrada; Senator Raul Roco; outgoing secretary of defense, Renato de Villa; Juan Ponce Enrile; Miriam Defensor-Santiago, running again; and Imelda Marcos, the wife of deposed dictator, Ferdinand Marcos. Imelda, however, had to withdraw from the race on April 29 after courts upheld her 1993 conviction and sentence on charges of graft. She threw in her support behind Estrada, who won by a majority of 30 percent of the votes.[26] Significantly, most votes cast for Estrada came from disaffiliated and poor people who grew poorer as a result of the recent economic crisis and dominant development processes.

PRESIDENT JOSEPH ESTRADA (1998–2001)

On May 11, 1998, Joseph Estrada was elected president, largely due to a devoted following among the poor masses, and was officially inaugurated into office by Congress on May 29. In his inaugural address, he promised to alleviate the conditions of poverty, fight crime, and eliminate corruption in government, especially corrupt officials in the military, bureaucracy, and judiciary.

Estrada was born Joseph Ejercito on April 19, 1937, in Manila. He was the son of a government engineer, and as a young man, he entered Ateneo de Manila University, where he failed to complete his studies. Subsequently, he went to Mapua Institute of Technology to pursue an engineering degree but eventually dropped out to take up a career in acting. He adopted the screen name of Joseph Estrada and went on to become a popular movie star who played the lead role in more than 100 films, usually as a John Wayne–type of hero who defended the weak and poor against the corrupt establishment. Estrada (nicknamed Erap) gained his following from the poor, mainly based on his movie persona as a tough guy hero with a big heart; he ran for president on the slogan "Erap, buddy of the poor." However, Estrada also had the support of friends; he received substantial financial backing from Imelda Marcos; her husband's cronies, especially Eduardo Conjuangco and Lucio Tan, the two richest men in the Philippines; as well as from a large group of wealthy Chinese Filipinos, perhaps hedging their bets in a bid to protect themselves from the ongoing syndicated spree of kidnappings, which disproportionately affected their community. As a result, Estrada was able to outspend his rivals in the presidential campaign. In addition, some progressive reformists and politically radical academics and intellectuals thought Estrada might help to further their cause on behalf of the poor and supported him for that reason.

Estrada began his political career in 1969, when he successfully ran for mayor of San Juan, where he served in this capacity until 1986. In 1987, he was elected to the Senate, where he helped to pass some agrarian reform legislation and voted against U.S. bases, which earned him some support from the Left and grass roots. However, once he assumed the presidency, Estrada's political image began to fade as he boasted of his many mistresses and surrounded himself with his gambling buddies and business and drinking partners. In the Philippines, access to the president is a great advantage, as all government contracts in excess of 50 million pesos require approval from the president.[27] Estrada was easy prey to his friends who approached him for his signature of approval on their deals. Estrada employed some of the same plunder techniques used by former President Marcos.[28] Corruption under the Estrada administration involved extending loans and extracting commissions from contracts, and the ownership of companies through nominees with such innovations as stock speculation (and manipulation) and the use of government pension funds for corporate merges and takeovers.[29] President Estrada began to fall from power starting in October of 2000 when his former gambling associate, a provincial governor, Luis Singson, reported that he had collected 414 million pesos, or about US$8.3 million, in bribes from illegal gambling syndicates, which he handed over to the president. There were other allegations, such as taking some US$12 million in bribes from *jueteng*, an illegal lottery; malfeasance in the use of national lottery funds that were earmarked for charities but never got there; and skimming funds from the tobacco tax. There were also allegations that Estrada used illegal earnings to purchase expensive mansions, sports vehicles, and luxury cars for his various mistresses and children.

Shortly after Singson's revelations broke, the opposition took steps to impeach President Estrada. Philippine Country Watch 2007, from which the following information derives, documented that more than 40 legislators resigned from both houses in a show of solidarity against the president. On November 13, the House of Representative sent a motion for Estrada's impeachment to the Senate. On December 7, the Senate began impeachment hearings on Estrada for bribery and corruption charges. On December 20, the impeachment court's presiding officer called for the investigation of a bank account with the Philippines third largest bank, Equitable PCI, in the name of Jose Verlarde, from which a check was issued for US$2.8 million. Prosecutors said Verlarde was a cover for Estrada, and a witness who worked in the bank came forward to testify that she saw Estrada sign the check.

By January 2001, however, the Senate impeachment trial lost momentum as the senators voted 11 to 10 not to open incriminating bank records, which brought the impeachment trial to a halt. Eleven senators resigned in disdain, as citizens went to the streets in a People Power II revolution demanding Estrada's resignation. The number of protestors grew to half a million, and on January 19, major military leaders and police joined them and put their support behind Vice President Gloria Macapagal for President. In a stubborn show of resistance, Estrada called his supporters among the poor masses to stage a large People's Power III rally in an effort to face down the opposition. On January 20, the armed forces withdrew their support from Estrada, and the Supreme Court declared "vacant" the presidency and then declared Vice President Macapagal Arroyo the new president. She was sworn into office the same day.

PRESIDENT GLORIA MACAPAGAL ARROYO (2001–)

Gloria Macapagal Arroyo was born on April 5, 1947, in San Juan, Manila, to Diosdado Macapagal and Evangelina Macaraeg Macapagal. Her father was the president of the Republic of the Philippines from 1961 to 1965, as mentioned in chapter 6. From autumn 1964 to spring 1966, Gloria studied economics at Georgetown University in Washington, D.C., and, after returning to the Philippines and graduating magna cum laude from Assumption College, she went on to earn her master's degree in economics at Ateneo de Manila University in 1978. That same year, she married Jose Miguel Tuason Arroyo. She earned her doctoral degree in economics at the University of the Philippines in 1986. From 1977 to 1987, she served as an assistant professor at Ateneo de Manila University and as a professor at the University of the Philippines School of Economics.

She was a still a university professor when President Corazon Aquino called on her to serve as undersecretary of trade and industry in 1986. Macapagal Arroyo won a seat in the Senate in 1992 and was reelected in 1995. In May 1998, she ran for vice president with Jose de Venecia, the presidential candidate of Lakas ng Tao, which was the leading party in Congress at that time. De Venecia lost to Joseph Estrada, but Macapagal Arroyo won the separate race for vice president. The former President Estrada appointed her to serve concurrently as secretary of social welfare and development. On January 20, 2001, as discussed in the previous section, Estrada was deposed from office, and Vice President Gloria Macapagal Arroyo became the 14th president of the republic.

On May 10, 2001, when the general elections were held, Arroyo easily won the presidency and carried a majority of the seats in the Senate and earned the loyalty of local officials. President Arroyo had to face significant social, economic, and political challenges, including how to win back the support of the poor, still supporters of Estrada. The poor masses voted in Estada's wife and the former police chief, Panfilo Lacson, to the Senate, and they voted in several other Estada cronies to the House of Representatives.[30] Also, Arroyo had to strategically maintain the support of her congressional majority if she were to push through her liberalization agenda, which included economic reforms that Estrada failed to implement, such as increasing privatization, especially of the national power company, and making the economy, which was based on trade and export, more competitive in the global market.

After the political crisis waned, some economic recovery occurred in the nation.[31] There was a significant rise in the gross domestic product, up 4.4 percent from the low of 3.0 percent in 2001, as well as an increase in remittances from Filipinos working abroad. However, on the downside, the poverty rate had gone up to 40 percent, up from 31.8 percent under the Ramos administration, and other social indicators of education, health, and welfare were dismal. President Arroyo had to service the national debt repayments, which consumed more than 25 percent of national budget in 2002.

Another matter that President Arroyo had to contend with was the issue of Muslim separatists in Mindanao, especially the Muslim separatist group led by Abu Sayyaf. CountryWatch Philippine Review for 2007 reports that President Arroyo, immediately, moved to curb the fighting between the armed forces of the Philippines (AFP) and Muslim rebels. Her government and the Moro Islamic Liberation Front (MILF) signed a cease-fire agreement. However, the kidnappings and other crimes being committed by the stray Abu Sayyaf group continued to increase. For example, on March 20, 2000, Abu Sayyaf abducted 23 teachers and 30 students, including Claretian missionary Father Rhoel Gallardo, in the southern Philippine island of Basilan. In the aftermath of the encounter between the government's soldiers and Abu Sayyaf terrorists, four hostages, including Gallardo and school teachers Anabelle Mendoza, Editha Lumame, and Ruben Democrito, were found dead.[32] In June 2001, Abu Sayyaf kidnapped 16 people from a central Philippine resort, and senior AFP military officers were indicted in the kidnapping and accused of helping the group escape in exchange for cash payment.[33] This revelation led to other accusations of high government officials being involved in corruption, such as in the national insurance system, among other bureaus. Abu Sayyaf received millions in ransom money from kidnapping, which the Philippine authorities believe has served to arm as well as embolden the rebels, although CountryWatch documents that the terrorist organization of Osama bin Laden has also been providing arms and logistical support to the Abu Sayyaf terrorists since the early 1990s.

After the 9/11 terrorist attacks in the United States, however, the fight against Abu Sayyaf was jettisoned to the forefront because his terrorist organization had been receiving substantial support, largely in the form of weapons and other military hardware, but also monetarily, from Osama Bin Laden, who was alleged to have been behind the bombing of the World Trade Center in New York City on September 11, 2001. The Philippines was one of the first governments to support U.S. President George Bush's war on terrorism, and President Arroyo deployed thousands of troops to fight against Abu Sayyaf in Basilan, where they were taking the hostages. Later, the U.S. military began to assist the AFP in pursuit of the Abu Sayyaf group. This move was looked on favorably by some Filipinos; however, it met with criticism from nationalist NGOs and people's organizations, and many nationalist intellectual elites who considered President Arroyo to be a puppet of the United States. The AFP continued to fight against internal "terrorists," those who used to be called "Communists": the New People's Army nationwide and the Moro Islamic Liberation Front, a fundamentalist splinter group from the earlier Mindanao National Liberation Front, in Mindanao. However, the effects of the war against terrorism in the Philippines has made the lives of citizens who are directly affected worse.

> The war, itself, can be regarded as terroristic, particularly in Mindanao, where the army has aggressively engaged the MILF and when the number of internal refugees at its peak rose to a half a million. In one period alone, from January to October 2002, according to the Ecumenical Movement for Justice and Peace, more than 9,000 civilians were victims of military assaults. Only now, with the cease fire between the government and the MILF in place, has the tide receded. However, most military en-campments lie in civilian areas, putting these residents in danger should hostilities resume. And the economic costs to both the government and the farmers, workers, and small entrepreneurs have been staggering— and this is in an area that has the country's five poorest provinces, all Muslim.[34]

On yet another front, President Arroyo tried to go after corrupt government officials, but her anticorruption drives, which were widely publicized, had the reverse effect, in some instances exposing the government's weakness in being able to enforce the law. For example, when she tried to clean up the Bureau of Internal Revenue (BIR), the bureaucracy responded by slowing down the collection of taxes and using its network in Congress, which resulted in further shrinking revenue. When the newly appointed commissioner of the BIR tried to rid the bureau of corrupt employees, he was sued by his own officers and finally resigned after a bomb was planted in his office.[35] President Arroyo faced many of the same obstacles as did her father, President Macapagal, when he tried to clean up corruption in the government.

Finally, she was elected to another six-year term in May 2004. Her opponents were Secretary of Education Paul Roco; Estrada's former police chief, Panfilo Lacson; Eduardo Villanueva of the Jesus Is Lord Movement; and aging action movie star, Fernando Poe Jr. However, Secretary of Education Paul Roco had to drop out for health reasons, and his camp threw its support behind Villanueva. Gloria's running mate, Noli de Castro, was elected vice president. Although opposition supporters claimed there was widespread election fraud and angry protestors marched on the presidential palace, they had to be dispersed by riot police who used water cannons against them. The opposition claimed that Arroyo's government was as repressive as the Marcos dictatorship, but she replied that it had to protect against anarchy. President Arroyo would continue to be plagued by problems resulting from the opposition. In 2005, she invited her critics to bring their complaints against her to Congress where she would submit herself to due process. That September, President Arroyo underwent an impeachment trial in the Congress and survived after the parliamentary body formally rejected the motion by the opposition. Arroyo's presidency was secured as a result of the hearings, and her government, though still vulnerable, continues in 2007 to enjoy political stability in face of the opposition.

NOTES

1. David Joel Steinberg, *The Philippines, A Singular and Plural Place* (San Francisco: Westview Press, 1990), pp. 5, 377.

2. Ed Rollins, *Bareknuckles and Back Rooms: My Life in American Politics* (New York: Broadway Books, 1996), cited in Robert Parry, "Huckabee's Chairman Hid Payoff Secret" in *OpEdNews*, p. 1, http://www.opednews.com/articles/genera_robert_p_07128_s_Chairman_htm.

3. David Joel Steinberg, *The Philippines, A Singular and Plural Place*, p. 171.

4. Amy Blitz, *The Contested State: American Foreign Policy and Regime Change in the Philippines* (New York: Rowman & Littlefield, 2000), p. 163.

5. These officers were mainly 1970 and 1971 graduates of the Philippine Military Academy, who served under and helped to implement Marcos's martial law regime. Colonel Gregorio Honasan was the most notorious leader of RAM.

6. David Joel Steinberg, *The Philippines, A Singular and Plural Place*, p. 150.

7. James Putzel, *A Captive Land, The Politics of Agrarian Reform in the Philippines* (Manila: Ateneo de Manila Press, 1992), p. 207.

8. *The Philippine Facts and Figures 2006* (Manila: National Statistics Office), p. 10.

9. James Putzel, *A Captive Land, The Politics of Agrarian Reform in the Philippines*, p. 206.

10. Robert Youngblood, *Marcos against the Church: Economic Development and Political Repression in the Philippines* (Ithaca: Cornell University Press, 1990), p. 179.

11. Ibid.

12. Walden Bello, Herbert Docena, Marissa de Guzman, and Marylou Malig, *The Anti-Development State* (Quezon City: Sociology Department, University of the Philippines Diliman; and Bangkok: Focus on the Global South, A Program of Development Policy Research, 2004), p. 22.

13. Clarke, Gerard, *The Politics of NGOs in Southeast Asia, Participation and Protest in the Philippines* (New York: Routledge Press, 1988), p. 3.

14. David Joel Steinberg, *The Philippines, A Singular and Plural Place*, p. 149.

15. Ibid.

16. Sonia Zaide, *The Philippines, A Unique Nation* (Quezon City: All Nations Publishing Co., 1999), p. 405.

17. Joel Rocamora, *Breaking Through: The Struggle within the Communist Party of the Philippines* (Pasig: Anvil Publishing, 1994), p. 174; excerpt in Patricio Abinales and Donna Amoroso, *State and Society in the Philippines* (New York: Rowman & Littlefield, 2005), p. 262.

18. Patricio Abinales and Donna Amoroso, *State and Society in the Philippines*, p. 245.

19. Mercado, Ruth, "Labor Updates, Gradual Pains," in *VIHDA Files*, Vol. 8, Nos. 10–11 (1992), pp. 3–4.

20. Maurice Godelier, *Rationality and Irrationality in Economics* (New York: Monthly Review Press, 1972).

21. Sonia Zaide, *The Philippines, A Unique Nation*, p. 409.

22. Peter Krinks, *The Economy of the Philippines, Elites, Inequalities, and Economic Restructuring* (New York: Routledge Press, 2002); cited in Patricio Abinales and Donna Amoroso, *State and Society in the Philippines*, p. 248.

23. Sonia Zaide, *The Philippines, A Unique Nation*, p. 409.

24. Patricio Abinales and Donna Amoroso, *State and Society in the Philippines*, p. 256.

25. Kathleen Nadeau, *Liberation Theology in the Philippines: Faith in a Revolution* (Westport, CT: Praeger Publishers, 2004).

26. Sonia Zaide, *The Philippines, A Unique Nation*, p. 410.

27. Patricio Abinales and Donna Amoroso, *State and Society in the Philippines*, p. 273.

28. Walden Bello, Herbert Docena, Marissa de Guzman, Marylou Malig, *The Anti-Development State*, chap. 7.

29. Walden Bello, Herbert Docena, Marissa de Guzman, Marylou Malig, *The Anti-Development State*, p. 262.

30. Patricio Abinales and Donna Amoroso, *State and Society in the Philippines*, p. 279.

31. Ibid.

32. Jose Torres Jr., *Into the Mountain: Hostaged by the Abu Sayyaf* (Quezon City: Claretian Publication, 2001).

33. Romeo Gacad, "Lamitan under Siege," and Ed Lingao, "Grease," In *The Investigative Reporting Magazine*, July–September 2001: 26–30, 31–34; cited in Patricio Abinales and Donna Amoroso, *State and Society in the Philippines*, p. 279.

34. Luis H. Francia, "Meanwhile in Manila," in *The Nation* (October 27, 2001).

35. Patricio Abinales and Donna Amoroso, *State and Society in the Philippines*, p. 280.

Notable People in Philippine History

Abu Bakhr, Sultan (ca. 1450). Sumatran religious leader who left Palembang for Sulu. He married Paramisuli (Malay *permaisuri:* "queen consort"), Rajah Baginda Ali's daughter. After his father-in-law's death, he established the sultanate of Sulu and became its first sultan.

Aguinaldo, Emilio (1869–1964). The president of the first Philippine republic (1899). He started as a member of the Magdalo Chapter of the Katipunan in Cavite, was elected president of the revolutionary government at the Tejeros Convention on March 22, 1897, and, later, Biak-na-Bato Republic. He proclaimed Philippine independence at Kawit on June 12, 1898. His capture foreshadowed the end of large-scale armed resistance to American rule. He ran against Quezon for the presidency of the commonwealth in 1935 but lost.

Aquino, Benigno, Jr. (Ninoy) (1932–1983). A senator and chief opposition leader during the martial law period (1972–1981), under President Ferdinand Marcos. Aquino's brutal assassination in 1983 galvanized popular opposition to the Marcos government and brought his widow, Corazon Aqino, into power.

Aquino, Corazon Cojuangco (1933–). Ninoy's widow who became president of the republic (1986–1992). With Salvador Laurel as running mate, she led the opposition that overthrew the authoritarian government of President

Marcos, who went into exile after the successful People's Power revolution of 1986. She first established a revolutionary government under the Freedom Constitution, later replaced by the Constitution of 1987, which served as the basis for reestablishing democracy.

Arroyo Macapagal, Gloria (1947–). Current president of the Philippines (2001–). She served as vice president under President Estrada and became president when he was forced to step down for malfeasance, through a People's Power II revolution. President Arroyo Macapagal has confronted some of the same obstacles as did her father, President Diosdado Macapagal, when he tried to clean up corruption in government. Her government continues to enjoy political legitimacy in the face of opposition.

Bonifacio, Andres (1863–1897). Supreme leader of the Katipunan, which he founded on July 7, 1892. He is considered the father of the revolution, for he perceived that Spain would not grant reform and that armed engagement was the only means to achieve national independence from Spain. He was tried and executed for sedition by the revolutionary government under General Aguinaldo.

Burgos, Jose (1837–1872). One of the three priests executed on February 17, 1872, for advocating the ordination of Filipino priests and transfer of the parishes to the dioceses. In his "Manifesto que a la Noble Nacion Espanola dirigen los leales Filipinos" (Manifesto addressed to the loyal Filipinos of the noble Spanish nation), Burgos identified his own people as not just natives but Chinese mestizos and Spaniards born in the Philippines as well as *Filipinos,* a new usage of the term at the time.

Del Pilar, Gregorio (1875–1899). One of the youngest Filipino generals in the Philippine Revolution and Filipino-American War. He commanded General Aguinaldo's rear guard during his retreat to northern Luzon and was killed in the battle of Tirad Pass (Ilocos Sur), on December 2, 1899.

Dewey, George (1837–1917). A U.S. naval officer who commanded the U.S. Asiatic Squad during the Spanish-American War.

Estrada, Joseph (1937–). A popular former action film star, who became president of the Philippines (1998–2001) but was arrested and stood trial at a congressional impeachment hearing on charges of accepting bribes and corruption. While this trial was aborted when the senators voted 11 to 10 not to open incriminating evidence against him, he was ousted from power anyway as a peaceful People's Power II revolution arose and called for his resignation.

Forbes, William Cameron (1870–1959). Known as the road-builder governor-general (1909–1959). In 1921, he became a member of the Wood-Forbes

Commission to investigate conditions in the Philippines. Forbes Park in Makati, Metro Manila, was named in his honor.

Garcia, Carlos Polestico (1896–1971). President of the Republic of the Philippines (1957–1961), remembered for his Filipino First Policy. He was among the founders of the Association for Southeast Asia (1963), the precursor of the Association for Southeast Asian Nations (ASEAN).

Gomes de los Angeles, Mariano/Gomez (1799–1872). One of the three secular priests garroted (1872) at Bagumbayan, now Rizal Park on Luneta Boulevard.

Harrison, Francis Burton (1873–1957). The governor-general (1913–1919) remembered for his Filipinization policy, replacement of Americans in the Philippine civil service with qualified Filipinos, thereby giving the latter the opportunity for self-governance. He was retained as adviser on foreign affairs by the Philippine government after independence in 1946.

Kolumbu (ca. 1520). King of Butuan who made the first known treaty with Spain. He was befriended by and navigated the way for Magellan to Cebu.

Kudarat, Mohammad Dipatuan (1619–1671). A sultan of Mindanao who united the people of Lanao, Cotabato, Davao, Sulu, Zamboanga, and north Borneo and was a staunch defender of the Islamic faith against Spanish Christian encroachments.

Lapu Lapu (ca. 1520). Warrior-king of Mactan Island (now part of Cebu Province). He was the first to successfully resist the Spanish and was responsible for the death of Ferdinand Magellan on April 27, 1521.

Laurel, Jose, Sr. (1891–1939). Secretary of the interior (1923); senator (1925–1931); delegate to the Constitutional Convention (1934); chief justice during the commonwealth. When World War II broke out, he was instructed by Manuel Quezon to stay in Manila and deal with the Japanese to soften the blow of enemy occupation. During the Japanese occupation, he served in various capacities and helped draft the 1943 constitution. He became president of the Second Republic (1943–1945). As president he defended Filipino interests and resisted Japanese efforts to draft Filipinos into the Japanese military service. Upon return of the American forces, Laurel was imprisoned in Japan when MacArthur occupied that country. He was returned to the Philippines to face charges of treason, but these were dropped when President Roxas issued an amnesty proclamation. In the Third Republic, he was elected senator and negotiated the Laurel-Langley Agreement.

Legazpi, Miguel Lopez de (1510–1572). First Spanish governor and captain general of the Philippines (1565–1572) who founded the first permanent settlement on Cebu. He was awarded the first *encomiendas* (land grants for collecting tribute) and made Manila the capital of the Philippines in 1571.

Lopez Jaena, Graciano (1856–1896). A revolutionary essayist and editor of *La Solidaridad*. Exiled in Spain due to his work as an orator and propagandist, he headed the group that established *La Solidaridad*.

Luna, Antonio (1866–1899). Commander-in-chief of the Army of Liberation of the first Philippine republic and brother of Juan Luna, the famous painter. He studied military strategy and tactics in Europe and was considered the best general of the Philippine-American War. He was assassinated by the followers of Pedro Alejandro Paterno (reformists for collaboration with the Americans) in Cabanatuan, Nueva Ecija, on June 5, 1899.

Mabini, Apolinario (1864–1903). Nationalist, statesman, lawyer, philosopher, and educator who became the chief adviser of Emilio Aguinaldo. He was regarded as the most brilliant Filipino mind of the revolutionary era. He also was known as the Sublime Paralytic because his legs were paralyzed.

Macapagal, Diosdado (1910–1997). President of the Republic of the Philippines (1961–1965). He asked Congress to pass the Agricultural Land Reform Code, which abolished share tenancy and installed a leasehold system in its place; it finally passed on August 8, 1963. This was a significant step toward resolving the agrarian problem. It was during his presidency that Independence Day was moved from July 4 to June 12, which was the date when General Aguinaldo proclaimed Philippine independence in Cavite.

MacArthur, Douglas (1880–1964). The army chief who became the youngest chief of staff of the U.S. Army and one of a half dozen officers who earned the five-star rank during World War II. He served as military adviser to the Philippine commonwealth with rank of field marshal (1936–1941). He was recalled from retirement to serve as the commanding general of the U.S. armed forces in the Far East, formed in 1941; he became the supreme allied commander in the southwest Pacific, 1942–1945, and supreme commander for Allied forces of occupied Japan in 1945–1951. His father was General Arthur MacArthur who commanded U.S. troops during the Philippine-American War.

Magellan, Ferdinand (1480–1521). A Portuguese navigator who circumnavigated the world in the name of Spain. He brought the attention of Europe to the existence of the Philippines. He was killed by King Lapu Lapu in the battle of Mactan.

Magsaysay, Ramon (1907–1957). Served as president of the Philippines (1953–1957). Formerly, he was President Quirino's secretary of defense who was instrumental is suppressing the HUK rebellion. As president, he persuaded

Congress to pass the Agricultural Tenancy Act (1954). It was during his term that the Retail Trade Nationalization Act was passed. He secured revisions in the Bell Trade Act and was the first president to revise the U.S. Military Bases agreement to bring it more in line with Philippine interests. He died in an airplane crash in March 1957 before his term as president ended.

Malvar, Miguel (1865–1911). Nationalist revolutionary general and farmer who is considered to be the last general to surrender to the Americans on April 16, 1902.

Marcos, Ferdinand (1917–1989). President of the Philippines (1965–1986) who declared martial law on September 21, 1972. After the People Power revolution in February 1986, he was ousted from power and lived in exile in Honolulu, Hawaii, where he died in 1989.

McKinley, William (1843–1901). President of the United States during whose term the United States intervened in the Cuban War against Spain and ended up purchasing the Philippines at the signing of the Paris Peace Treaty in 1898. He sent the Schurman Commission in January 1899, followed by the Taft Commission in 1900, the latter of which was instrumental in organizing a civil government to replace the military government, which had been in existence since 1898.

Osmena, Sergio, Sr. (1878–1961). The first Filipino national leader under the American regime as speaker of the Philippine assembly and the second president of the Philippines (1944–1946).

Paterno, Pedro (1857–1911). The Filipino intellectual writer and negotiator of the truce pact of Biak-na-Bato (1897). He was president of the Mololos Congress (1898) and Apolinario Mabini's successor as prime minister of the Mololos Republic (1899). He was also a member of the reform movement that advocated for collaboration with the Americans and author of the novel *Ninay* (1885).

Quezon, Elpidio (1890–1956). As vice president during Manuel Roxas's term, he was also secretary of foreign affairs and became president when Roxas died in 1948. He was elected president in his own right in 1949.

Ramos, Fidel (1928–). He was president of the Philippines from 1992 to 1997. As head of the Constabulary, under President Marcos, he was instrumental in helping to design and implement martial law. Together with General Ponce Enrile and the RAM, he defected from the government in 1986 and joined forces with the People's Power revolution that ousted Marcos from power. His presidency is remembered for better integrating the national economy in the global scheme.

Rizal, Jose Protacio (1861–1896). National hero of the Philippines who authored two revolutionary novels, *Noli Me Tangere* (1887) and *El Filibusterismo* (1891). Rizal helped to inspire the Filipino Propaganda Movement and was one of the main ideologues of Filipino nationalism. He was executed at Bagumbayan, now the Rizal Park, on December 30, 1896.

Roosevelt, Franklin Delano (1882–1945). President of the United States (1933–1945). His presidency was noted for the New Deal during the Great Depression. Roosevelt tried to keep America out of the war in Europe and the Pacific, while attempting to aid Great Britain against Germany, but the United States entered the global conflict after the bombing of Pearl Harbor.

Roosevelt, Theodore (1858–1919). President William McKinley's vice president, who became president when McKinley was assassinated in 1901. He tried to regulate big-business monopolies through the Sherman Anti-Trust Law. He served as governor-general of the Philippines from 1932 to 1933.

Roxas, Manuel Acuna (1892–1948). He was the last president of the Philippine commonwealth and the first president of the republic (1946–1948).

Salazar, Bishop (ca. 1580). First Roman Catholic bishop of the Philippines, who, in 1581, called a synod to address the issue of early Spanish abuse of Filipinos.

Sin, Jamie Cardinal (1928–2005). Archbishop of Manila from 1974 to 2003. He helped to restore democracy by playing a leading role in the People's Power revolution that ousted the dictator Ferdinand Marcos from power through nonviolent means.

Taft, William Howard (1857–1930). First American civil governor of the Philippines (1901–1904); secretary of war (1904–1908); U.S. president (1909–1913); U.S. chief justice (1921–1930). Designed and helped to implement early U.S. policy of co-opting the Filipino elite to join the government; they have been in power ever since.

Taruc, Luis (1913–2005). One of the founders of the Hukbalahap in 1942. He was its supremo until 1954 when he surrendered to government authorities.

Twain, Mark (1835–1910). He was one of the leaders of the Anti-Imperialist League in the United States, who reported on the Filipino-American War on location from the Philippines. He was also a popular humorist and fictionist who wrote under penname of Samuel Langhorne Clemens.

Wood, Leonard (1860–1927). The American governor of Sulu known for the massacre of Muslims in Bud Dajo in 1906. He served as the governor-general of the Philippines from 1921 to 1927.

Yamashita, Tomoyuki General (1885–1946). Japanese army general during the war in the Pacific. He was sent in December 1940 for six months to Germany to observe front line Nazi blitzkrieg technique, which he applied in his speedy capture of Malaya and Singapore. He was then assigned to the Philippines on September 9, 1944, arriving two weeks before General MacArthur's first attack in his Philippine military campaign. Yamashita was captured, tried for war crimes, and hanged.

Zamora, Jacinto (1835–1872). One of the three priests who championed the secularization of the parishes in the nineteenth century. Together with Fathers Mariano Gomez and Jose Burgos, he was executed by means of the garrote at Bagumbayan field (now Rizal Park, Luneta Boulevard) on February 17, 1872.

Glossary

AFP: Armed forces of the Philippines

alipin: Precolonial Tagalog rubric for two categories of slaves know as *nama-mahay* (tribute payers) and *gigilid* (household servants)

ASEAN: Association of Southeast Asian Nations

aswang: Generic term for vampire witches

barangay: Boats used by the *datus* to sail to the Philippines; term used by Spanish to refer to precolonial local communities of 30–100 families; under Spanish and American colonizers, *barangay* became barrio or village government, although *barangay* is still used interchangeably with barrio to refer to village government

BIR: Bureau of Internal Revenue

bolos: Long single-edged machete

Cha Cha: Charter Change; a constitutional convention to amend the constitution

CIA: Central Intelligence Agency

civilian guards: citizens used by the AFP in cooperation with the U.S. CIA to fight against antigovernment groups after World War II; since 1988, referred to as CAFGU, citizens armed forces geographical units

conquistadores: Spanish military leaders who established Spanish rule

datu: Malay word for "lord"; title of nobility prevalent among precolonial Filipinos

encomenderos: Spanish officers who were granted land and people, *encomiendas*

encomiendas: Settlements made by the Spanish for purposes of collecting taxes and tribute from the local people

friars: Spanish term for Roman Catholic priests

gigilid: Precolonial Tagalog term for household slave

GNP: Gross national product

Green Revolution: The development of high yielding varieties of rice and cereals; the International Rice Institute based in Manila has been active in the Green Revolution

HUK: Hukbong Bayan laban sa Hapon or Hukbalahap (People's Anti-Japanese Army or People's Liberation Army)

illustrados: Intellectual class; the Filipino educated elite

indios: Term used by the Spanish to refer to the early indigenous Filipinos

jueteng: Illegal lottery

JUSMAG: United States–Republic of the Philippines Military Group

Katipunan: Radical revolutionary association founded by Andres Bonifacio on July 7, 1892, to fight for Philippine independence from Spain

KBL: Kilusang Bagong Lipunan (New Society Movement)

kris: Short sword or heavy dagger with a blade; ceremonial sword of the Muslims

LDP: Laban ng Demokratikong (Struggle of the Democratic Philippines)

Liga Filipina: Secret association founded by Jose Rizal on his return to the Philippines in 1892 to prepare his fellow country men and women for independence from Spain

Mahabharata: Two-thousand-year-old Hindu epic of the origination of the world/India

mestizo: Spanish term for the offspring of Chinese and Indio or Spanish and Indio couples

MILF: Moro Islamic Liberation Front, a fundamentalist splinter group from the MNLF

MNLF: Mindanao National Liberation Front (also Mindanao National Independence Movement), a revolutionary movement for an independent Muslim republic consisting of Mindanao, Sulu, and Palawan

namamahay: Precolonial Tagalog term for tribute payers of the *alipin* (slave) class

NAMFREL: National Association for the Maintenance of Free Elections

NGO: Nongovernmental organization; a nonprofit, cause-oriented organization

NPA: New People's Army, the armed branch of the Communist Party of the Philippines

Philippine 2000: economic development program of President Fidel Ramos

principalia: Local landed officials under Spanish rule paying land taxes; only landed elites paying taxes could vote (and they voted only landed, tax-paying elites into office)

rajah: Hindu political title used in precolonial Southeast Asia; rank equivalent to *datu*

RAM: Reform the Armed Forces Movement

reconcentrados: Concentration camps; armed surveillance of local populations

salvaged: Arbitrary and unlawful abduction, torture, and execution of political dissenters and suspected criminals by the military and paramilitary

sayyid: Honorific title that signifies decent from the prophet Muhammad

snap election: Term used by President Marcos when he announced without prior notice that he was going to hold an election

sultan: Islamic title for ruler or king

sultanate: A Muslim political state ruled by a sultan

timawas: Precolonial Tagalog term for commoners or free persons

USAFFE: U.S. armed forces in the Far East

Bibliographic Essay

General histories of the Philippines written by Filipino scholars are *The Philippines: A Unique Nation* by Sonia Zaide (Quezon City: All Nations Publishers, 1999) and *State and Society in the Philippines* by Patricio Abinales and Donna Amoroso (New York: Rowman & Littlefield, 2005). Renato Constantino's *The Philippines, A Past Revisited (pre-Spanish–1941)* and *The Philippines: A Continuing Past (1941–1965)* are classic texts written from an insider's perspective. For a history of the rise of Islam in the southern Philippines, there is Cesar Adib Majul's *Muslims in the Philippines* (Quezon City: University of the Philippines Press, 1999). A highly useful reference book is the *Cultural Dictionary for Filipinos*, edited by Thelma Kintanar and associates (Quezon City: University of the Philippines Press and Anvil Publishing, 1996).

Comprehensive histories of Southeast Asia and the world that situate the Philippines are *Slavery, Bondage, and Dependency in Southeast Asia* by Anthony Reid (New York: St. Martin's Press, 1983); *Asian and African Systems of Slavery*, edited by James Warren (Berkeley: University of California Press, 1980); *When China Ruled the Seas* by Louise Levathes (Cambridge: Oxford University Press, 1994); and, last but not least, *Over the Edge of the World* by Laurence Bergreen (New York: Harper Perrenial, 2004). A particularly profound and detailed account of early European expansionism in the region is *The Cradle of Colonization* by George Massleman (New Haven: Yale University Press, 1963).

There is an extensive bibliographic storehouse from which to draw for early Philippine history. A major body of these sources is the historical documents that have been compiled and published in five collections, *colecciones de documentos ineditos* (collections of unpublished documents), by the Spanish government from 1825 to 1932. Another collection written in Spanish that is still ongoing is *Historia de la Provincia Agustiniana del Smo. Nombre de Jesus de Filipinas* by Isacio Rodriguez. There are other primary materials, published and unpublished, such as chronicles, travelogues, navigational logs, letters, missals, sermons, catechisms, reports, and dictionaries. Early dictionaries are especially important, for the information therein provides a glimpse into the sixteenth-century social and cultural life of the islanders. However, non-Spanish speakers, such as this author, have had to rely on English translations of primary documents. One of the earliest collections written in English is Blair and Robertson's *The Philippine Islands, 1493–1898,* which consists of 55 volumes. This classic historical reference, albeit from a Western perspective, can be found in Filipinana library collections in the Philippines (e.g., University of San Carlos Library in Cebu City) as well as in research universities with extensive Philippine studies collections in the United States and elsewhere. An excellent rendition of ancient Philippine society as told from the perspective of the Jesuit missionaries that provides a wellspring of information for the discerning reader is *The Jesuits in the Philippines, 1581–1768* by H. de la Costa, S. J. (Cambridge: Harvard University Press, 1961).

Two histories that assess the persistence of ancient Philippine cultural influences in the face of Spanish colonialism are *Pasyon and Revolution: Popular Movements in the Philippines, 1840–1910* by Reynaldo Ileto (Quezon City: Ateneo de Manila University Press, 1989) and *Contracting Colonialism: Translation and Christian Conversion in Tagalog Society under Early Spanish Rule* by Vicente Rafael (Ithaca: Cornell University Press, 1988). There are historical inquiries into the issue of colonization and changing constructions of sex and gender, such as "Collision of Cultures: Historical Reformulation of Gender in Lowland Visayas, Philippines" by Cristina Blanc-Szanton in *Power and Difference: Gender in Island Southeast Asia,* edited by Jane Atkinson and Shelly Errington (Stanford University Press, 1990), and *Colonizing Filipinas, Nineteenth Century Representations of the Philippines in Western Historiography* by Elizabeth Mary Holt (Manila: Ateneo de Manila Press, 2002). No study of early Philippine history would be complete without reading some of the many works of William Henry Scott, such as *Cracks in the Parchment Curtain and Other Essays in Philippine History* (Quezon City: New Day, 1982), *Prehispanic Source Materials for the Study of Philippine History* (Quezon City: New Day, 1984), *Slavery in the Spanish Philippines* (Manila: De la Salle University Press, 1991), and *Barangay* (Manila: Ateneo de Manila Press, 1994).

The colonization of the Philippines by the United States (1898–1946) in tandem with the nationalist independence struggle has been extensively covered. This period has been examined in Philippine history books mentioned at the outset. Another exemplar is *Filipinos and Their Revolution* by Reynaldo Ileto (Manila: Ateneo de Manila Press, 1998). Aside from these informative works, there are texts on the role of religious leaders, including *Revolutionary Clergy: The Philippine Clergy and the Nationalist Movement, 1850–1903* by John Schumacher, S.J. (Manila: Ateneo de Manila University Press, 1981); *Revolutionary Spirituality, A Study of the Protestant Role in the American Colonial Rule of the Philippines, 1898–1928* by Mariano Apilado (Quezon City: New Day, 1999); and *The Church and Its Social Involvements in the Philippines, 1930–1972* by Wilfredo Fabros (Manila: Ateneo de Manila Press, 1988). A thoughtful analysis of the rise of Muslim separatism in the Philippines is *Muslim Rulers and Rebels* by Thomas McKenna (Berkeley: University of California Press, 1998). A classic study on the HUK, the early forerunner of the Communist/Socialist movement, is *The HUK Rebellion: A Study of Peasant Revolt in the Philippines* by Benedict Kerkvliet (Berkeley: University of California Press, 1977).

There are a numerous historical accounts of the American conquest and takeover of the Philippines, and its aftereffects, such as *Benevolent Assimilation* by Stuart Creighton Miller (New Haven: Yale University Press, 1982); *Mark Twain's Weapons of the Weak, Anti-Imperialist Writings on the Philippine American War* by Mark Twain, collated and edited by Jim Zwick (New York: Syracuse University, 1992); and *The Philippine Reader, A History of Colonialism, Neocolonialism, Dictatorship, and Resistance*, edited by Daniel Schirmer and Stephen Rosskamm Shalom (Boston: Southend Press, 1987). While all of these accounts illustriously explore the motives of the U.S. colonial regime and those who have resisted it, of special note is Schirmer and Shalom's collective work because it brings into its analyses documentary selections from such diverse sources as the CIA and the State Department, Presidents McKinley and Reagan, Philippine leaders including Aquino, Philippine nationalists and progressive organizations, and U.S. opponents to the American intervention. Another laboriously documented ethnography that takes a more conservative look at the American colonial government is Frank Hindan Golay's *Face of Empire, United States–Philippine Relations, 1898–1946* (Manila: Ateneo de Manila Press, 1997).

The post-independence period has been the subject of some meticulous and outstanding scholarship. The republic, during and after World War II, is exceedingly well documented in *The Philippines* by Jean Grossholtz (Boston: Little, Brown and Company, 1964) and "The Philippines" by David Wurfel in *Governments and Politics in Southeast Asia*, edited by George McTurnan Kahin (Ithaca: Cornell University Press, 1964). This period is also covered well in most general histories specific to the Philippines, such as *The Philippines: A Unique Nation* by Sonia Zaide (Manila: All Nations Publishing, 1999); *State and Society in the Philippines* by Abinales and Amoroso (New York: Rowman and Littlefield, 2005); and *The Philippine Reader, A History of Colonialism, Neocolonialism, Dictatorship, and Resistance,* edited by Daniel Schirmer and Stephen Rosskamm Shalom (Boston: Southend Press, 1978). The economic development of the country can be understood in relation to the governmental design and implementation of agrarian change polices in the nation that, largely, were put in place after World War II. Comparatively, these policies were influenced and shaped differently by collaborating local elites and U.S. policy makers based in the Philippines, Japan, and Korea, immediately after the war. Their different development paths are clearly articulated and explained in *A Captive Land, The Politics of Agrarian Reform in the Philippines* by James Putzel (Manila: Ateneo de Manila Press, 1992).

The Marcos regime has been given a great deal of attention after its demise, in titles such as *Waltzing with a Dictator* by Raymond Bonner (New York: Random House, 1987); *In Our Image, America's Empire in the Philippines* by Stanley Karnow (New York: Ballantine Books, 1989); and *America's Boy* by James Hamilton-Paterson (London: Granta Books, 1998). For an account of the development of underdevelopment of the Philippine economy during the Marcos period, there are the following resources: *The Philippines, The Political Economy of Growth and Impoverishment in the Marcos Era* by James Boyce (Honolulu: University of Hawaii Press, 1993); *Unequal Alliance, 1976–1986: The World Bank, the International Monetary Fund, and the Philippines* by Robin Broad (Manila: Ateneo de Manila Press, 1988); and *Development Debacle: The World Bank and the Philippines* by Walden Bello, David Kinley, and Elaine Elinson (San Francisco: Institute for Food and Development Policy, 1982). In addition, the role of the churches in countering authoritarianism has been documented in *Marcos Against the Church, Economic Development and Political Repression in the Philippines* by Robert Youngblood (Ithaca: Cornell University Press, 1990), while that of the NGOs is examined in *The Politics of NGOs in South-East Asia, Participation and Protest in the Philippines* by Gerard Clarke (London: Routledge, 1998). Continuities and changes reverberating through the republic in the post-Marcos era are well accounted for in *The Philippines: A Singular and Plural Place* by David Joel Steinberg (Boulder: Westview Press, 1990) and *The Contested State, American Foreign Policy and Regime Change in the Philippines* by Amy Blitz (New York: Rowman & Littlefield, 2000). Finally, while this list is representative, not exhaustive, of all the assiduously detailed accounts of Philippine history, a few more informative texts are *The Philippines: After Marcos,* edited by R. J. May and Francisco Nemenzo (London: Croom Helm, 1985); and *From Marcos to Aquino, Local Perspectives on Political Transition in the Philippines,* edited by Benedict Kerkvliet and Resil Mojares (Manila: Ateneo de Manila Press, 1991).

Index

Ramos, Fidel, 94, 99, 100; economic development plan of, 100–102, 103

Rizal, Jose, 33, 39, 40, 42. *See also Liga Filipina*

Roman Catholic Church: critical collaboration of, 89; social activism of, 89

Roxas, Manuel, 58, 67, 68

Salvaged, definition of, 93

Samar, American military campaign against, 53

Schurman Commission, 50

Shamans: early female, 35; Spanish vilification of, 35

Sin, Jamie Cardinal, Archbishop, 91, 94

Slavery: ancient Asian, 7; China, 10–11; Philippines, 11–12; in Thailand, 8–9

Southeast Asia, definition of, 1

Spain: colonial rule over the Philippines, 33–35; colonial system of, 27–30; and galleon trade, 33–34; revolution against, 38. *See also* Christianity

Spanish-American war, 42; and Philippine revolution against the United States, 43

Spanish mestizos, 39

Spanish revolution, 34

Sri Vijaya, 5–4

Sugar barons, on Negros Island, 61

Sulu sultanate, 7. *See also* Bakhr, Abu

Taft, William Howard, 44, 50, 51

Taft commission (second), 50

Tagalogs: early, 17–18; and Islam, 17

Trade: ancient maritime system of, 1, 3–7, 19; galleon, 33–34; with medieval Europe, 19

Traditional hierarchy, 3–6, 16, 27; chiefdoms, 11; Datus, 16, 17; Spanish destruction of, 18, 27, 36

Treaty of Paris (1899), 44, 45

Treaty of Tordesillas (1943), 20

Tribute, 5

Tydings-McDuffie Act. *See* Philippine Independence Act

United States: business interests in the Philippines, 44; and colonization of, 42, 54; and repression of nationalist movements, 52. *See also* HUK

USAFFE (United States Armed Forces in the Far East), 58

Vietnam War, and Clark Air Base, 85. *See also* Marcos, Ferdinand

Visayas, 51

Wet rice cultivation, 2

Woods Forbes commission, 56

World Bank, 97

About the Author

KATHLEEN NADEAU is Associate Professor of Anthropology at California State University. She is author of *Liberation Theology in the Philippines: Faith in a Revolution* (Praeger, 2002).